D0240243

Sainsbury's

GARDEN LOG BOOK

Contents

Published exclusively for
J. Sainsbury plc
Stamford Street, London SE1 9LL
by Cathay Books
59 Grosvenor Street, London W1

First published 1984

ISBN 0-86178 290 9

Printed in Hong Kong

Text written by Anne de Verteuil
Drawings by Russell Barnett

Introduction

There can be few pastimes as exciting and rewarding as making your own garden and watching it grow, and it's a challenge open to anyone with a patch of soil and a bit of time. There is no mystique to gardening; it is essentially a practical business and, once you have understood something about the way a plant works and what it needs from its environment to make it productive and keep it healthy, there is no substitute for getting your hands dirty, experimenting, observing and learning from the results.

With this in mind, The Garden Log Book is intended as both a practical handbook of advice and information and a useful working record of your own experiences of gardening.

The book is divided into three main parts, with a number of blank pages and charts for your notes in each. The first, Planning Your Garden, deals with the whole process of designing and making a garden, with suggestions for organizing and making best use of the space, timing and planning the work and some of the basic tools you will need.

Part two, The Plant Guide, deals with the plants themselves and contains a guide to some of the many cultivated plants available, with details of seasonal performance, particular requirements and so on, plus a section on the main garden pests and diseases.

Part three, The Gardener's Year, is a practical calendar: the 'How to' and 'When to' of the main tasks and operations throughout the gardening year.

Use the blank pages at the back for noting down the addresses of suppliers, nurseries and garden centres and any particularly interesting gardens that you have visited. Whether your garden is a back yard or an acre, it is hoped that you will find The Garden Log Book useful and that you will enjoy using it.

PLANNING YOUR
GARDEN

This is a step-by-step guide to the business of designing and planning a garden from scratch. The notes should also be helpful if you have recently acquired an established garden or are simply thinking of ways to improve your own.

The planning process is divided into three parts: 'What You Have and What You Want' tells you how to analyze all the factors which influence your garden and assesses its advantages and drawbacks.

'Making Decisions' involves the more complicated task of how to achieve what you want within the limitations. Every garden has its own particular problems and features and every gardener his own notions of what constitutes the ideal garden. The finished product should be an expression of your own personality, not merely a patchwork of borrowed ideas.

'Getting Down to Work' deals with how to time the work and gives brief notes on a few individual planting areas.

Each section has a grid on which you can draw up plans of your garden at the different stages in its development, and blank pages for notes.

Where you live

North or south: As a rule the climate is more extreme in the north of the country. Spring comes later, frosts are more persistent, winters harder, rainfall heavier. This will affect the range of plants you can grow successfully.

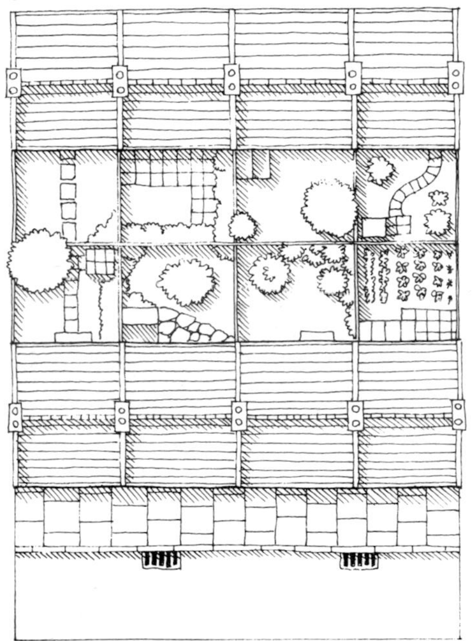

Town or country: Cities offer a more protected environment for plants, but the degree of pollution in the atmosphere might make you think twice about growing vegetables. Consider the many plants that tolerate and even thrive in city conditions.

Hillside or valley: On a windswept hillside you might need to think about planting to form a shelter or windbreak around the garden, but you will be less troubled by standing water or frosts, which tend to drain down into the valley. If your garden is very exposed, choose low-growing plants, such as alpines, or plant taller plants in a sheltered position near a wall.

What you have

Aspect: Which way do you face? Make a note of where the sun rises and sets in relation to your garden. This will affect the relative amount of sun and shade a particular area gets over the year, as well as during the course of a day, and this in turn will affect how you use the space. Surrounding buildings and trees will block light and cast shade, but also provide shelter.

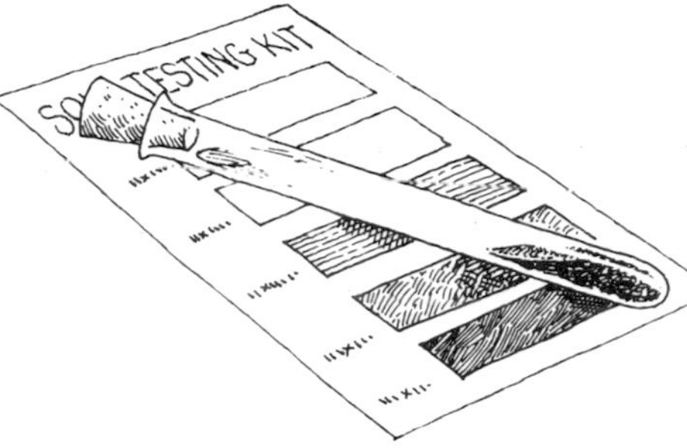

Soil: The geology of your particular part of the country will have an influence on the kind of soil you can expect to find in your garden. The following chart gives the characteristics of the five main soil types and how to treat them. The typical garden soil is a mixture of the various types and may even vary in different parts of the garden; by walls and close to the house, for example, there may be a higher lime content because of the presence of brick and mortar.

The acid/alkaline extremes are known as the pH of the soil. Based on a scale which runs from 0–14 is neutral, above is alkaline, below acid. The best garden soil is usually taken to be 6.0–7.5, on the acid side. Simple soil-testing kits are available which help you determine the acid/alkaline content.

Soil types

Sandy: Large, loose particles, light in colour and texture. Retains warmth. Easily worked. Good drainage. Deficient in nutrients.	**Improvement:** Add regular dressings of manure and compost; small frequent dressings of lime (not at same time).
Clay: Tiny particles bound together. Stiff and sticky when wet. Cold and hard to work. Poor drainage. Cracks in dry weather. Often acid.	**Improvement:** Add grit or coarse sand for drainage. Well-rotted manure, compost, peat into topsoil. Apply lime to surface.
Chalky: Contains lime – alkaline. Pale in colour, possible lumps of chalk. Fast drainage: shallow topsoil tends to dry up in droughts. Lime-hating plants will show signs of chlorosis (yellowing leaves).	**Improvement:** Frequent additions of compost and manure to topsoil. Mulch with peat to retain moisture.
Peaty: Acid. Soft, spongy, dark and crumbly. Excellent moisture retainer, no clogging. Use on clay soils. Lime-hating plants thrive.	**Improvement:** Possible lime dressing to balance extreme acidity.
Loamy: Balanced combination of sand and clay. High proportion of humus (decayed organic matter). Warm, well-drained, full of nutrients. Light loam: predominance of sand. Heavy loam: predominance of clay.	**Improvement:** Correct acidity with lime, or alkalinity with compost, to give medium loam – the perfect growing medium.

What's already there

These are the contents of your garden, the things you can change and the things you are stuck with: permanent structures, paved areas, features, trees and plants, as well as landmarks outside which affect your views or light.

If the garden is new to you, the kind of plants and how they grow can tell you a lot about the soil and its condition. Note also those areas where nothing grows, not even weeds.

What you want
Put all these limitations aside and consider what you want your garden to be and how you are going to use it. Is it to be a place to sit and relax in or a place to work? Do you want a labour-saving garden or do you have enough time to grow vegetables and keep an herbaceous border? Do you have children? Are you elderly or disabled? Do you want a shed, a greenhouse, a paved area for barbecues? Sort out your main needs and requirements and any particular features you would like to include and think about whether what you want and what you need are compatible. Space may make it impossible to meet all your ambitions.

Cost
Lack of space may not be the only thing that foils your plans. The expensive items in any scheme will be any hard materials, such as brick or paving, and the cost of labour unless you are prepared to do the work yourself. If the house is yours, you may also want to take into account its value and how much it is worth spending on the garden.

Time
Closely related to 'how much' is 'how long'. How long will it take to achieve your plans? How long are you likely to be in the house? Planting takes time to establish – it may be two or three years before the garden looks full. You might think about interplanting the slower-growing trees and shrubs with fast-growing species (which could be removed later). Plan carefully to avoid unnecessary expense.

Legal points and your neighbours
The upkeep of boundaries can be a vexed subject. Find out who is responsible for walls and fences – the wall on one side may be yours, on the other side your neighbour's. You don't normally need planning permission for free-standing constructions, but it's worth checking first. Inform or consult your neighbour before embarking on work that may affect him, interfere with his drains, or his access to light. This would include planting a large-growing tree where it will overhang his sunniest spot. In conservation areas you may need permission to cut down a tree, even in your own garden.

Measuring up and drawing the plan
It will probably now help you to collect all this information together and draw up a plan of the garden in its present state. The following blank pages include a grid for your plan and space to enter details of garden use, aspect, soil, etc.

Using a tape measure, take accurate measurements of the length of the garden boundary walls and house wall and draw these up in position on your plan using an appropriate scale. Now mark on N,E,S,W and the exact position of any features, buildings, trees, large shrubs or noteworthy plants. Show also the extent to which outside trees overhang your garden and use arrows to show views you want to keep or screen. Help make decisions by marking areas you feel positively about + and areas/views you feel negatively about –.

Plan of Existing Garden

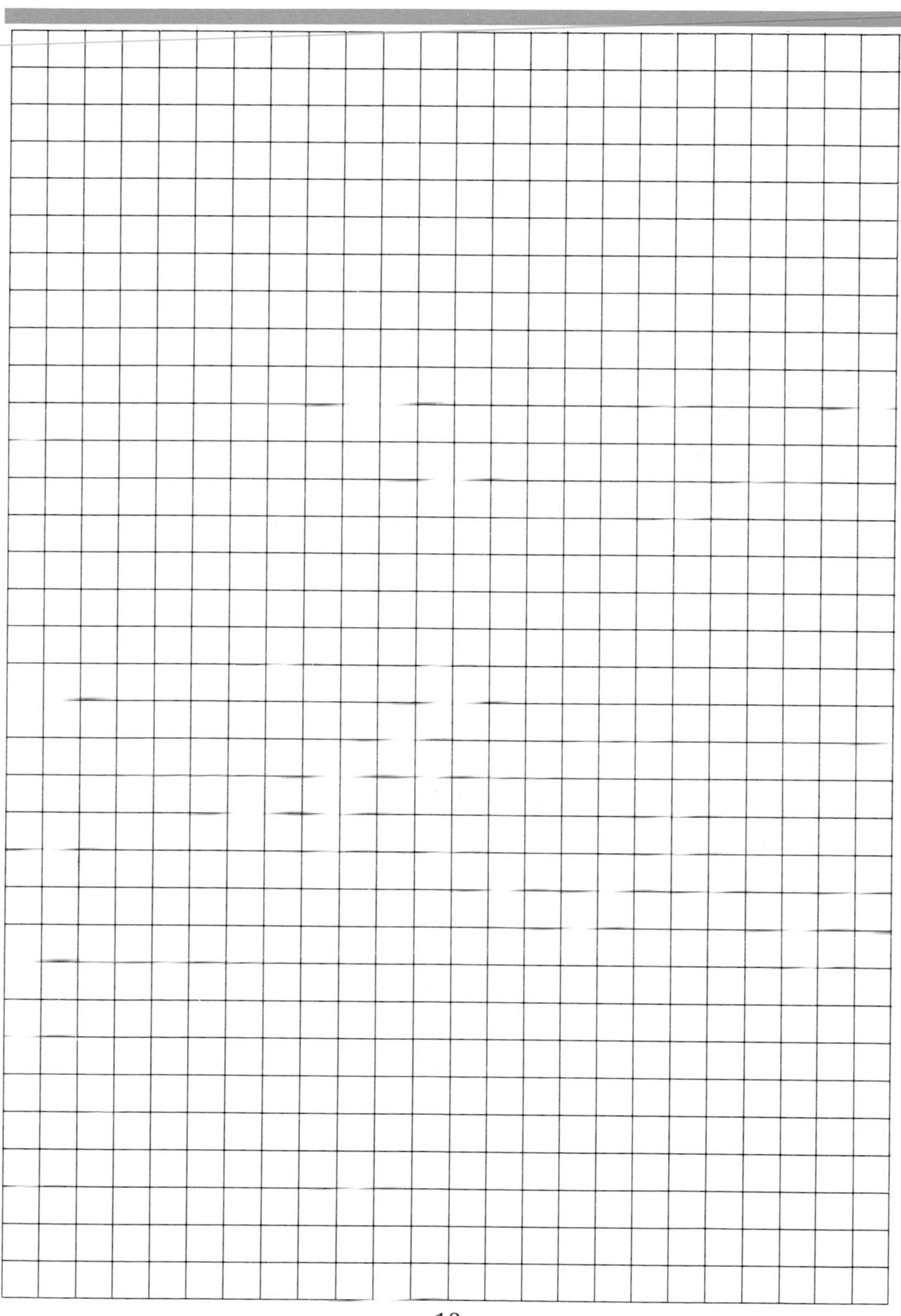

What You Have

Using this page as a written key to your plan, make headings for the different areas and note under each relevant information about soil, sun/ shade, objects you want to move or screen, plants which are doing particularly well, etc.

What You Want

Make notes here on how you are going to use your garden, features you feel are essential (lawn, shed, etc) and features you would like to include.

Making Decisions

Analyzing the exact limitations of your garden is important, but can be depressing. You have to reverse the process and begin to build on the positive aspects, exploring the possibilities open to you within the limitations. But where do you start?

Think of the whole garden
First, stop thinking of the garden as a series of separate areas, some good, some bad. Think of it instead as a whole – as it will be seen from the back door of your house. Think in very general terms about what you can see from there and about which views you particularly want to keep or screen.

Think vertically
Although you may have already made some of these decisions on your plan, remember that the plan is an aerial view which shows how parts relate to each other on the ground but gives no idea of height or depth. When you look at your garden you will be looking at plants and structures of varying heights as well as flat stretches of lawn or paving.

The character of your garden
Every garden has its own atmosphere which comes from a combination of factors: the surroundings, the way it faces, the things in it, your house. Getting the feel of it and interpreting the atmosphere is what will give it character and make it your own. Choose materials which are in sympathy with the style and character of house and garden.

The following guidelines are some suggestions as to how you can make the most of your space and get round certain obstacles.

Your garden in relation to its surroundings
If when you look out at your garden all you can see are other buildings, your first consideration may be how to screen them. If the building is another house, a simple solution would be to fix trellis panels on the back wall or fence and grow a screen of climbers.

If the building is a large block of flats, this probably won't have much effect. Planting tall shrubs or trees at the bottom of the garden will actually emphasize what you are trying to hide, by pointing right up at it. Think instead of diverting the eye down into the foreground of your garden, drawing attention away from the background.

Screening
As a solution to this kind of problem you might plant a small spreading tree or construct a timber framework or pergola for climbing plants, close to the house. This will have the effect of focusing attention on a feature which is attractive in its own right and interrupts the view.

Scale in the garden
The size of the plants you choose should suit the garden itself. Avoid using heavy, large-leaved shrubs in a small area – they will dominate and look out of proportion.

Size and shape of the garden

The most successful gardens are those in which everything is not obvious at first glance. Concealing certain areas and revealing others is a way of making a garden interesting and inviting. You could take a tracing of your plan and experiment with different ways of hiding and minimizing the negative areas by emphasizing and opening up the positive ones.

The following notes deal with some of the commonest problems of shape and size:

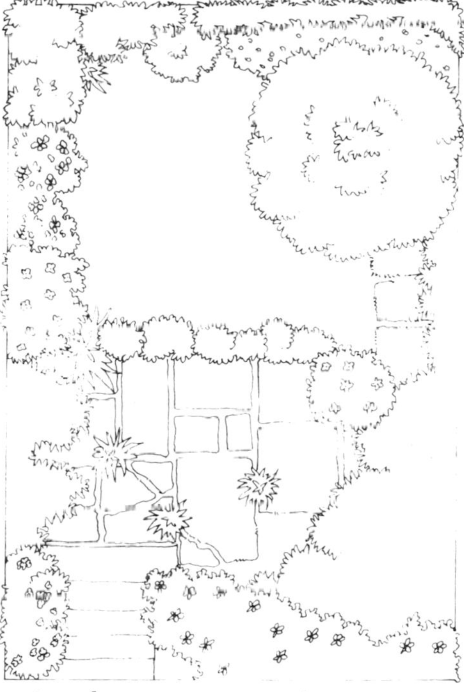

In a long narrow garden increase the depth of planting at the back and perhaps divide the space across its width into two or more areas which lead into one another. You can do this literally with trellis screens or arches or suggest it with planting or a paving pattern which runs from side to side.

In square and rectangular gardens avoid running straight beds along all sides. Break up the shape by curving planting beds or bringing some areas of planting into the centre, so that there are hidden areas behind.

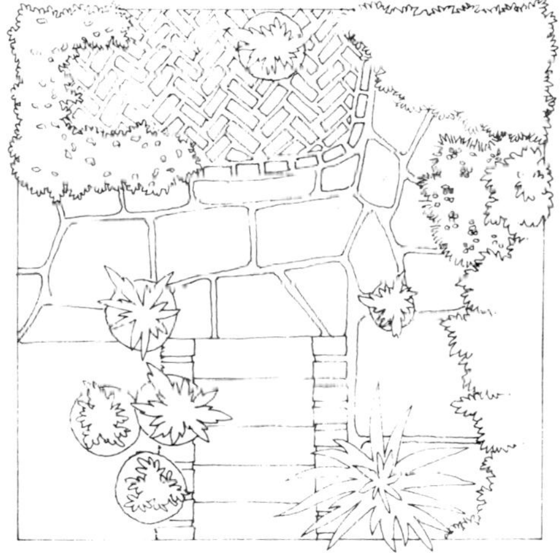

In small areas which can't be divided horizontally, think about dividing the space vertically, by introducing planting at different levels: climbers and hanging-baskets as a backdrop, with raised beds or pots and containers set at different heights.

Other tricks
Positioning larger objects and plants in the foreground, smaller objects and plants further back will make the back boundary appear further away. Bright colours (reds, yellows, oranges) will dominate the eye and leap forward; pale colours (greens, blues, white) will recede into the background.

Getting down to details
By now you should have a good idea of how you are going to use the space and have probably made rough decisions about what you want and where.

If not, now is the time to define the main areas and decide what proportion of space to give to each. General headings are lawn or paving, working areas, planting areas. Some of the decisions will already have been made for you by what's in the garden and where the areas of sun and shade are.

Lawn or paving
Choose a sunny position, allow enough space for a table and chairs if possible or a climbing frame if you have children. In a very small space a lawn can be a nuisance, particularly if you don't have room to store a lawn mower. Paving might be a better solution. Gravel provides a cheap and very attractive alternative and plants can be grown in it. Not a good idea for families with children and dogs.

The working area
Shed: Usually best at the bottom of the garden; don't use up valuable sunny space. You could disguise it with climbers, but make sure you can get in through the door.
Greenhouse: Needs a sunny position (see 'The Greenhouse').

Compost: Do you really have enough space or enough suitable stuff to feed it with? (See September, 'Gardener's Year'.) If so, put it in the shade but not against a wall.

Vegetable plot: Needs full sun and quite a lot of space to make it worthwhile.

Path: Useful for dry and easy access to working areas. Make it wide enough to take a wheelbarrow or lawn-mower, at least 1 m (3 feet). Can divide a garden. Paving slabs laid as stepping stones in the lawn are a good alternative in a small space.

Features and planting areas

Water: Best in a shady position, but not directly under a tree because of the leaves. Unless covered, can be a hazard to small children.

Trees: Check on their eventual size and spread before planting – they could create more shade than you can afford. Don't plant willows or poplars close to the house.

Plants: These are generally the most adaptable features in the garden. Some like full sun, some will grow in partial or complete shade. Some climb, some sprawl, some are upright, some spread. For now, concentrate on the shape of the beds and the general effect you want.

Thinking ahead

Before you draw in your plan of the garden as it will be, think carefully about the implications of your decisions.

Levelling an area which is raised may mean getting rid of a lot of earth. Do you have a side entrance or will it have to go through the house? You may need a skip.

Topsoil is very expensive and you might think of using soil from one area that you are levelling to make a raised bed somewhere else. Bear in mind that you may have to build a retaining wall with drainage holes to support the earth.

Raising an area may cause other problems where there are established trees. If there is going to be a big difference in soil level, you may need to protect the tree by building a wall around it.

If you are paving an area, do not cover existing manholes or drainage outlets. Allow a slight slope for water to run off towards the drains.

Draw in your projected plan on the next two pages.

Projected Plan

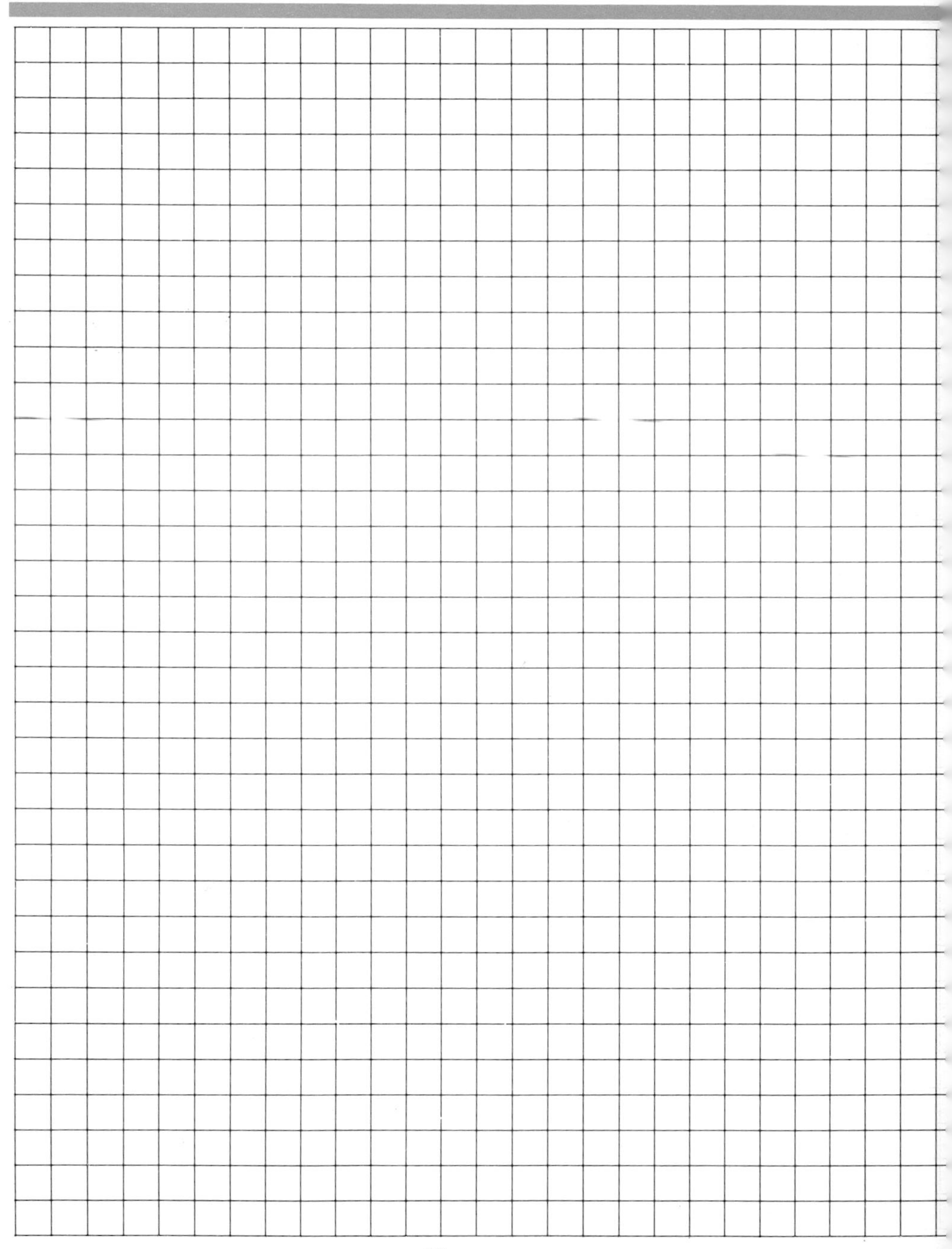

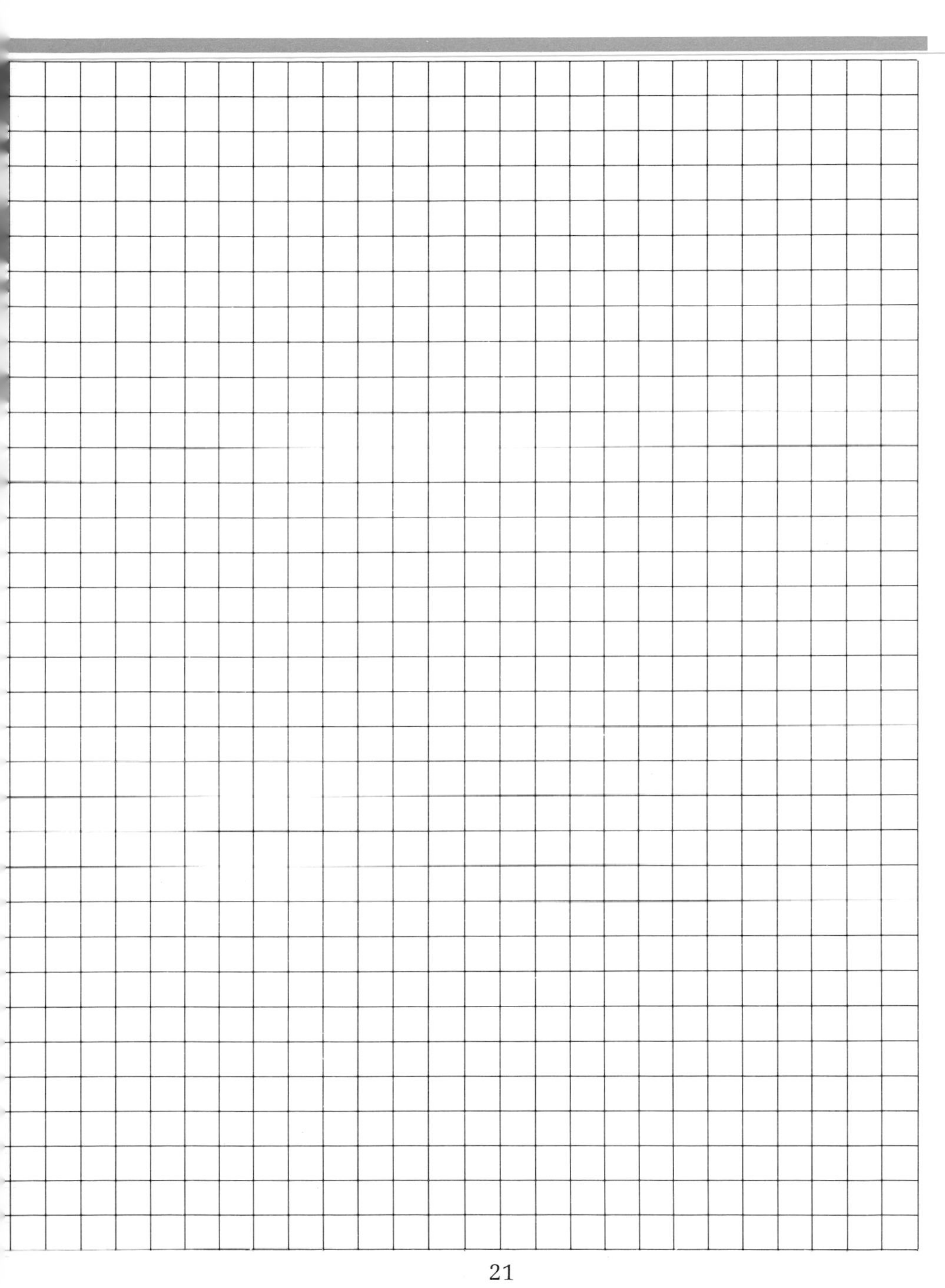

Getting Down to Work

Once you have settled on your plan, you will need to think about timing the work and the order of events.

Paving or structural work should be done first, if at all possible, to avoid damaging lawns and plants. Not in frosty weather.

Lawns are best sown in March or August (see April 'Gardener's Year') and not in dry spells. Protect the seed bed against birds. Turf is best laid in autumn or spring and, again, not in dry spells.

Planting container-grown plants can be done pretty well throughout the year, but spring and autumn are the main planting seasons. Make sure you place orders well in advance. Don't plant in very dry hot weather. Prepare planting beds in advance, if possible, correct any soil deficiencies and weed thoroughly.

Planting areas

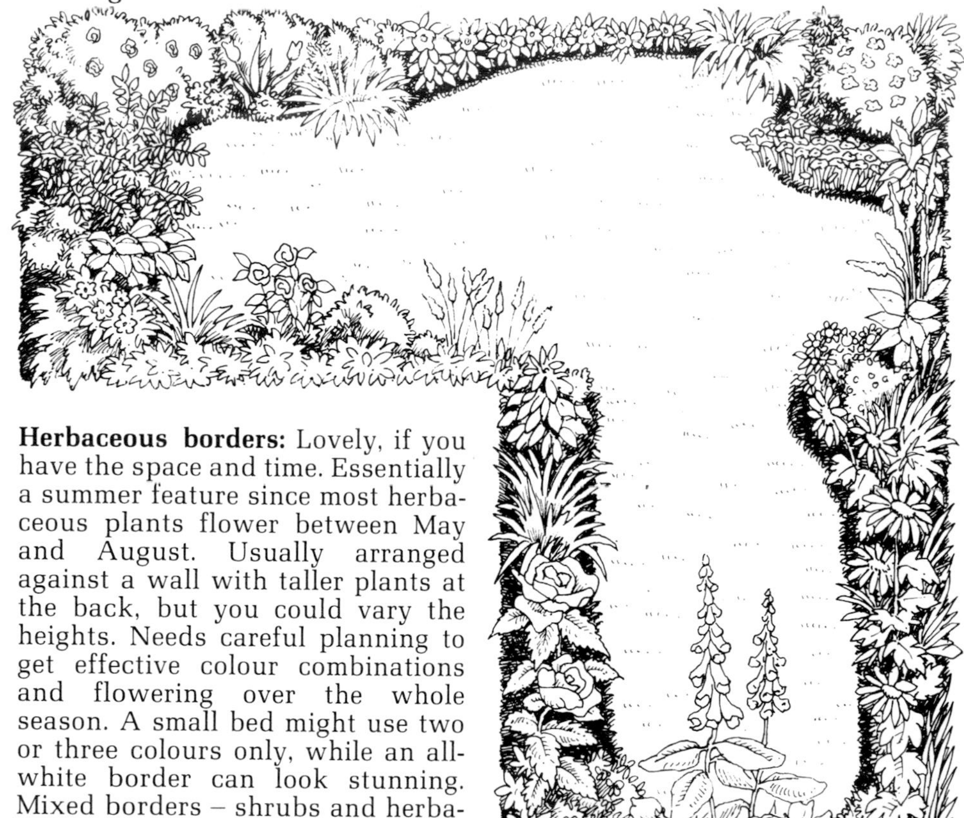

Herbaceous borders: Lovely, if you have the space and time. Essentially a summer feature since most herbaceous plants flower between May and August. Usually arranged against a wall with taller plants at the back, but you could vary the heights. Needs careful planning to get effective colour combinations and flowering over the whole season. A small bed might use two or three colours only, while an all-white border can look stunning. Mixed borders – shrubs and herbaceous together – require less attention and are better in a small garden for year-round interest.

Walls and fences: Make the most of these for growing climbers and wall shrubs. Provide good support in the form of wires or trellis for those that need training. Walls, particularly south and west-facing ones, offer protection for the more tender species. Small alpines will grow in dry stone walls. Some ferns will grow in brick.

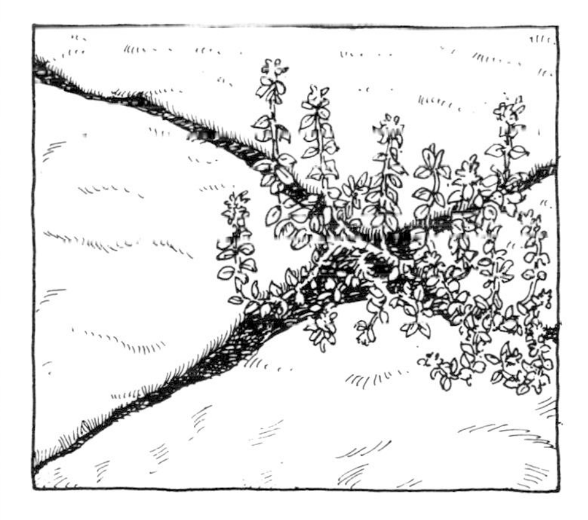

Paving: Loose-laid paving with soil in the joints looks very pretty planted with creeping thymes, acaena, trifolium repens.

Rockeries: A useful way of using boulders and attractive stones in the garden, if done with style. Rock plants need a dry, sunny position and really good drainage. Work grit into the soil and incorporate leaf-mould. Plant densely to avoid a weed hill and, when buying, distinguish between lime-lovers and lime-haters.

Peat beds: A way of growing lime-hating plants in limy soil. Can be built as raised beds, filled with peaty soil, with retaining walls made of peat blocks which must be kept moist otherwise they shrink. Partial shade is therefore the best position for these beds. Alternatively, fill beds or tubs with soil which contains a high proportion of peat.

Raised beds: A good way of dealing with excess soil and of introducing different levels. Makes gardening easier for the elderly and disabled. A well-built retaining wall is essential. Never build directly on top of paving without providing thorough drainage into the soil. In very small spaces keep height down to avoid foreshortening the space.

Herb beds: Lovely and useful close to the house. Need full sun and good drainage. Formal arrangements can be very effective, grown in squares or rectangles, bordered with a dwarf hedge of box or santolina, etc. Plant pockets of herbs in a sunny area of paving, by lifting a slab here and there.

Vegetable patches: Need space to be fully productive, full sun and a rich soil. Many vegetables are very decorative – ornamental brassicas and globe artichokes look striking in borders.

Pergolas: These and other structures, like arches, are lovely features for supporting climbing plants such as Wisteria and climbing roses. Treat the timber. Wire arches can be bought ready made.

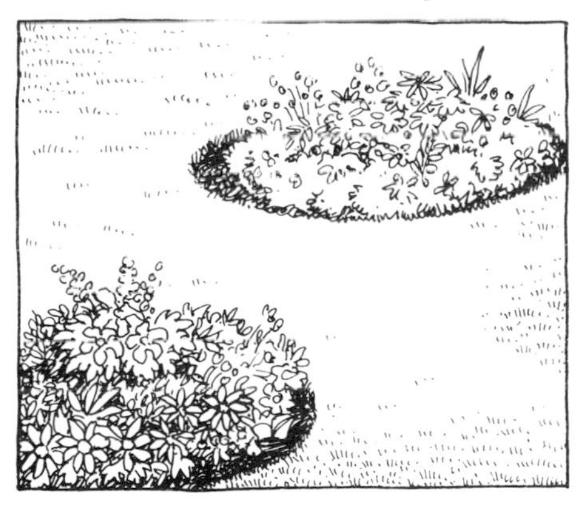

Island beds: Really only suitable for large gardens with spacious lawns. Edge beds to prevent grass invading.

Water gardens: A subject on its own. There are many ways of constructing a pool, from waterproof fabric and glass-fibre shells to concrete. Essential to make sure it is completely water-tight. Position in a sheltered spot. Aquatic plants can be grown in special baskets or pockets. Keep free of leaves and algae.

Under trees: Problem areas of dry shade. Use small ground-cover plants like Lamium, Vinca and variegated ivies which will rapidly cover the area. In rich soil, clumps of bluebells are lovely.

Planting Plan

On the following pages, make headings for the planting areas you want to include and list under each the kind of plants you want to grow there, including shape, height, colour, etc. For example, Bed on North-facing Wall: tall, screening climbers, shade-tolerant shrubs, evergreen, winter-colour, and so on. Also list any features which require particular kinds of plants, such as rockery, pergola, water.

Then, draw up your finished plan again on pages 30–31, showing the position and details of existing plants you want to keep and new plants as and when you decide on them. Indicate the plants with circles, drawn roughly to scale. If space is limited, number the circles and make a key on pages 32–33.

Planting Plan

Planting Plan

Planting Plan

Planting Plan

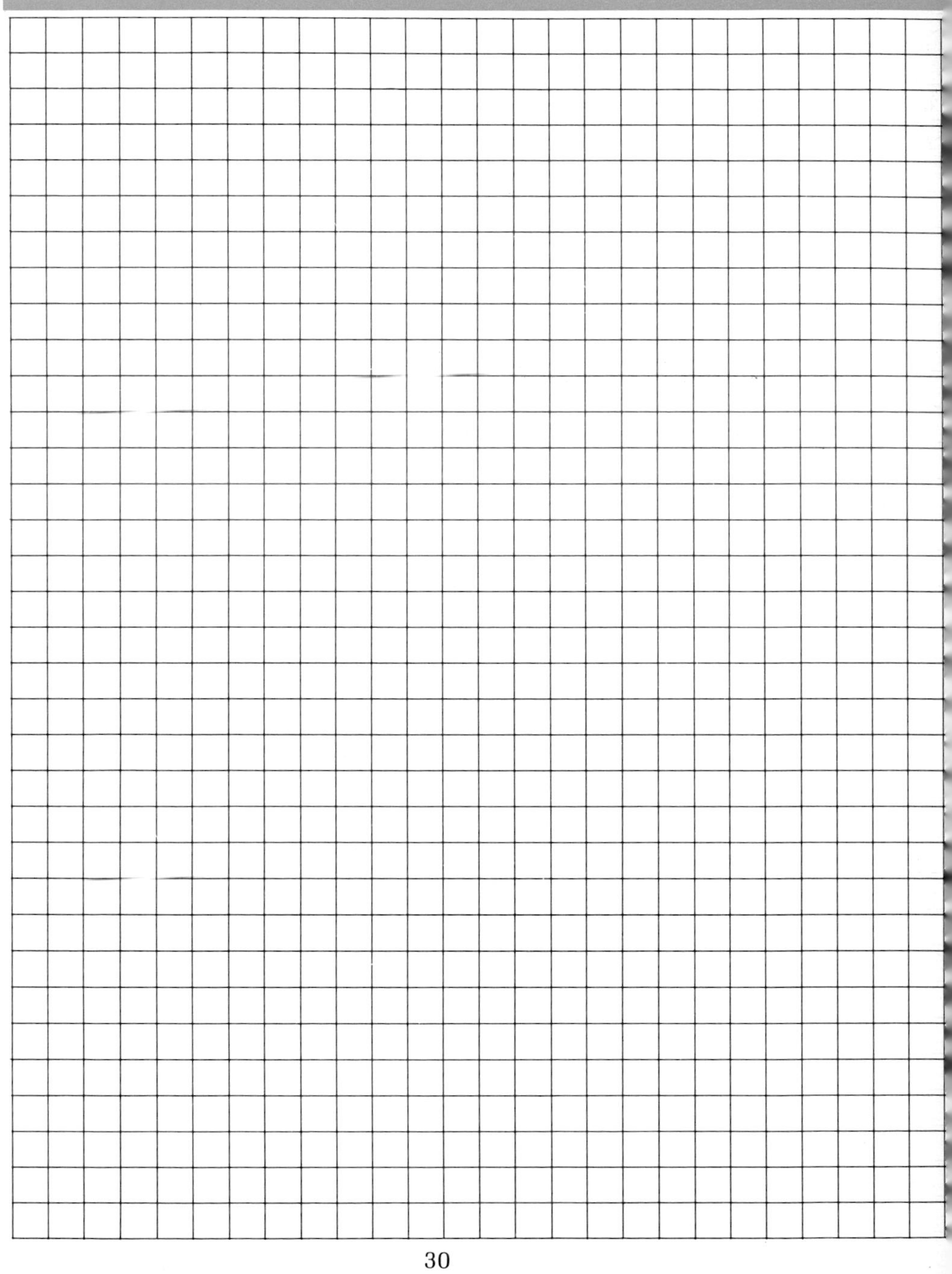

Key to Plants

Key to Plants

Basic Equipment

The range of garden hardware is extensive and can be bewildering. As a rule, buy the best you can afford: good, sharp-edged tools will make the job quicker and easier and will wear better. Look after them well. Clean all tools after use and put away. Scrape off mud or wash, wipe dry with cloth or oiled rag. Keep blades and edges sharp and rust-free.

The following tools are essential.

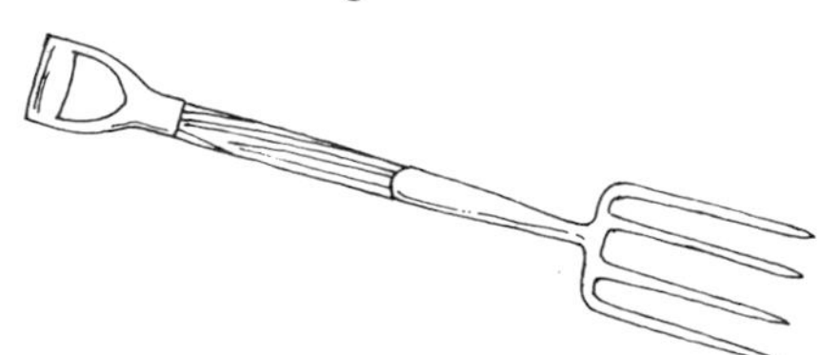

Large fork *for digging. D-shaped handle, with square prongs for lifting plants, round prongs for digging. Smaller size 'lady's' fork less heavy.*

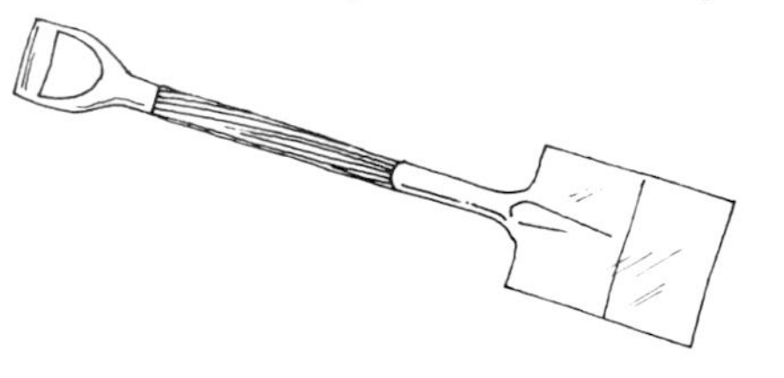

Large spade *for digging. D-shaped handle with square-ended blade. Stainless steel has a better cutting edge, is lighter to use and easier to maintain, though more expensive.*

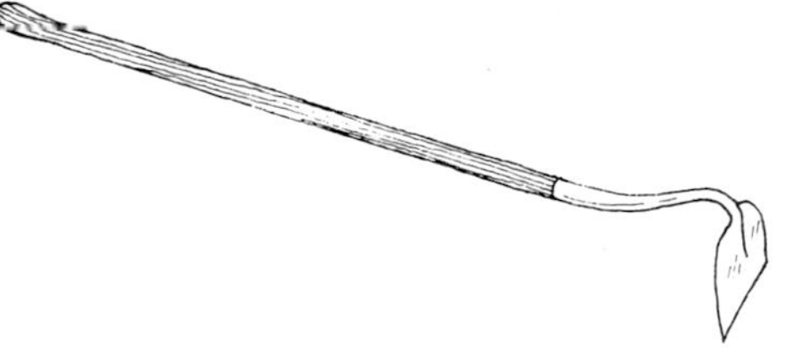

Dutch or draw hoe *(long-handled) for weeding. Dutch hoe: walk backwards, using push and pull acion. Draw hoe: draw towards you, slicing weeds. Stainless steel gives a good cutting edge.*

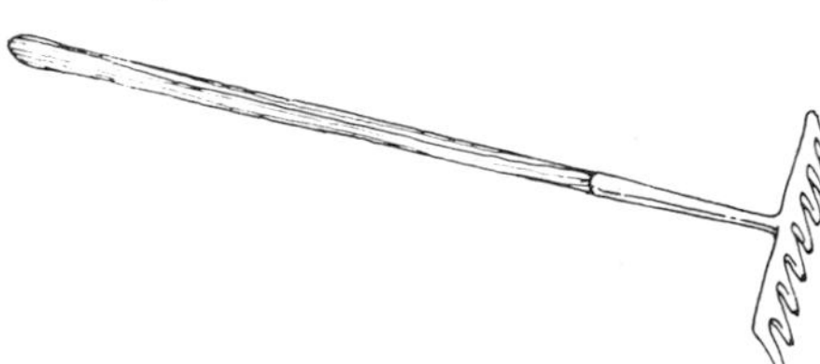

Metal rake *for levelling and getting soil to a fine tilth. Comes in different widths.*

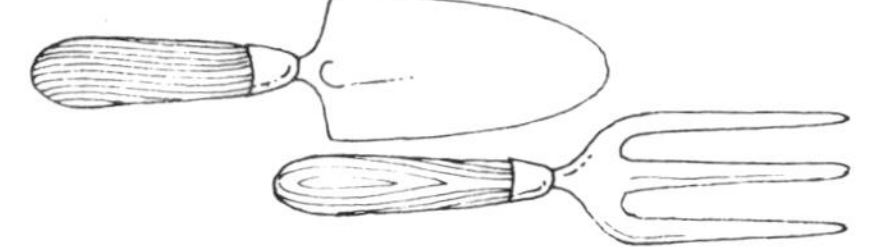

Hand fork and trowel *for close work, weeding, and planting small plants and bulbs.*

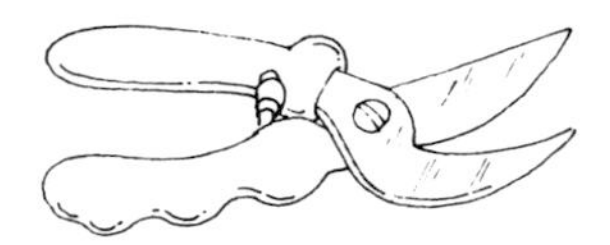

Secateurs *for cutting and pruning. Buy the best; keep blades sharp and rust-free.*

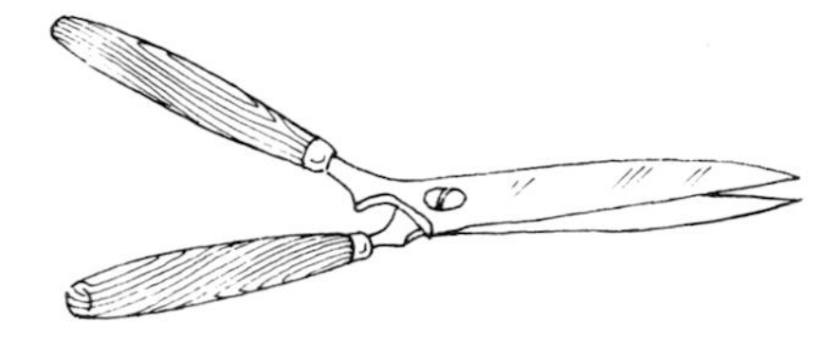

Shears *for trimming hedges and grass. Keep blades sharp so as to avoid 'chewing' plants. There are long-handled shears with angled blades for trimming lawn edges.*

Lawn mower *may be hand-driven (roller or side-wheel) or power-driven (cylinder or rotary action). Which you choose will depend on the size of your lawn and how much you are prepared to spend.*
Watering can *with fine rose for watering seedlings. Galvanized metal or plastic. If using for weedkiller, wash out thoroughly.*

Yard broom *for sweeping and clearing up paved areas.*

Springback or wire rake *for fallen leaves.*

Any or all of the following are well worth having too:

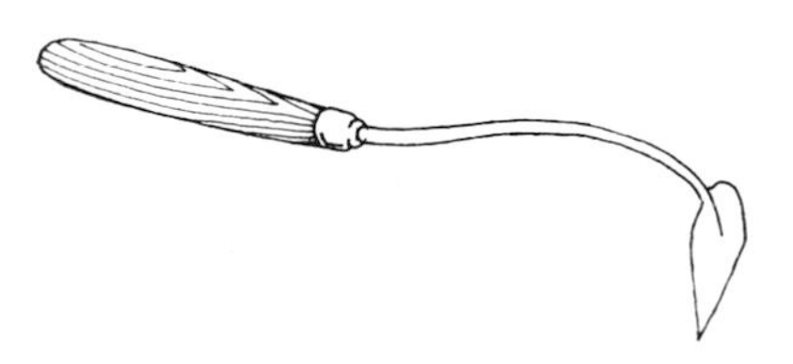

Hand or onion hoe *(short-handled) for close weeding.*

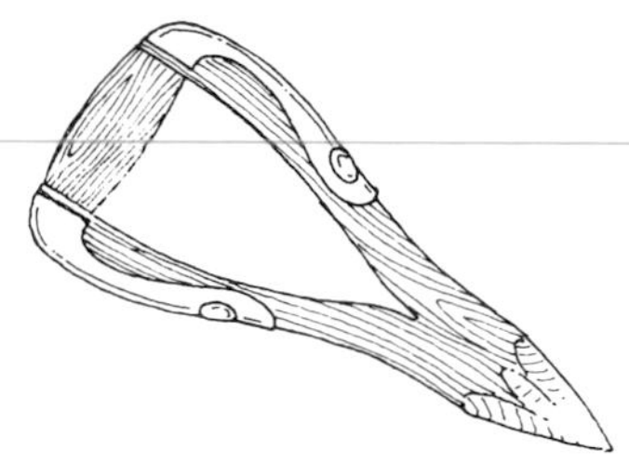

Dibber *for planting seedlings and small plants.*

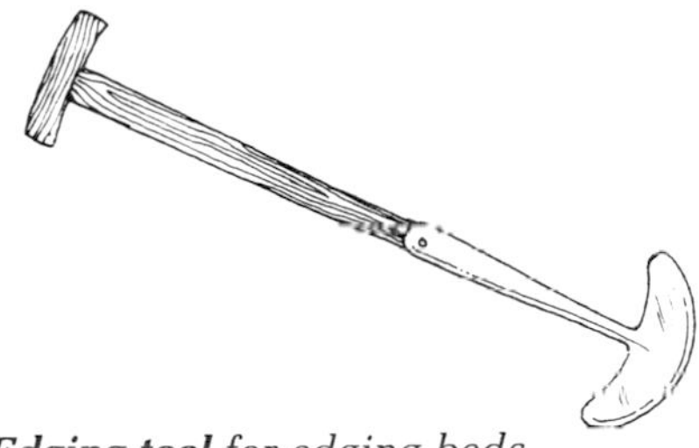

Edging tool *for edging beds.*
Hose *with rose spray and/or sprinkler attachment.*

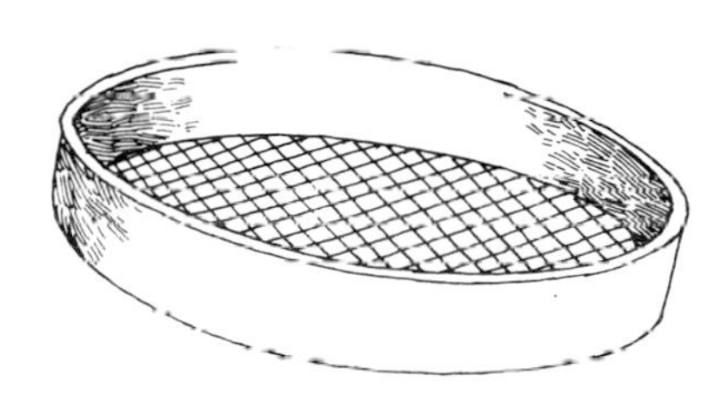

Sieve *for getting rid of stones and preparing seed beds.*
Garden line *(or twine and pegs) for measuring and sowing lines.*

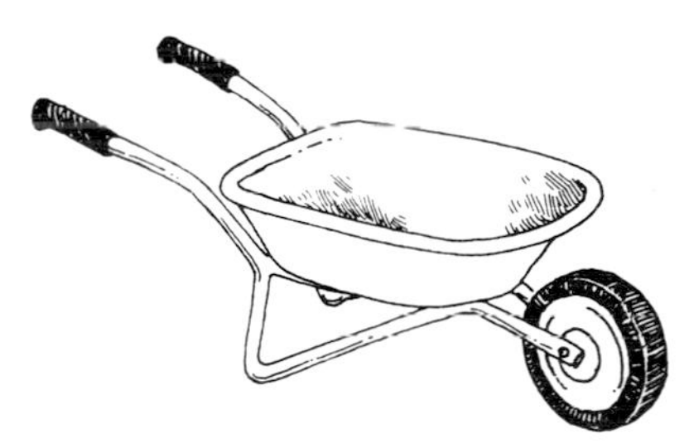

Wheelbarrow *for clearing and transporting soil, compost, etc.*

Checklist of Equipment

It may help to keep a record of what implements you have and where and when you bought them.

Implement	Where and when purchased

Implement	Where and when purchased

The Greenhouse

Greenhouses are available in a variety of shapes, sizes and materials. They may be full-glazed or half-glazed with wood, brick, metal or plastic walls. The wood and brick-walled types, though more expensive, conserve heat better than the metal or plastic types, which will be an important consideration if you want year-round use.

Siting the greenhouse
Position your greenhouse in full sun if possible – certainly never in dense shade or under trees. Ideally, shelter from north and east winds and have the ridge running from north to south. A lean-to structure against a south-facing wall is a good solution for a small garden. Hexagonal shapes are decorative and adaptable; the large area of glass admits maximum light, but also means greater heat loss than in the conventional ridge type.

Heating
Running a 'cool' greenhouse for year-round use means maintaining a minimum temperature of 7°C (45°F). There are various methods of heating, from paraffin and natural gas to electricity. Electric heating is obviously more expensive, but with a fitted thermostat is more easily controlled and takes up less space.

Ventilation and humidity
Adequate ventilation is essential – a certain degree of humidity is what to aim for. To obtain the warm moist conditions needed by germinating seeds, cuttings and those plants which normally grow in a warm climate, increase ventilation and 'damp down' – that is, spray plants, shelving and floor with water. In very hot weather this may need to be done two or three times a day. A humidity guage will be helpful. In early spring, autumn and winter, when the atmosphere is moister, keep plants on the dry side. You can still ventilate during the day in fine weather, but avoid draughts. Close down in very cold weather.

Light
Another essential, which is why siting the greenhouse is so important. Blinds or shades will guard against scorching in high summer and sharp frosts in winter.

Cleanliness
Keep all surfaces scrupulously clean, especially in summer when the risk of pest attack and infection is greatest: the humid conditions are perfect for pests as well as plants. Watch for and spray regularly against aphids, thrips, red spider mite and fungal diseases. Clear away all decayed and diseased material.

Using the greenhouse
Even a greenhouse without heating can be useful for bringing on seedlings early in the year and growing hardy plants and vegetables. With some heat it is an ideal place to propagate half-hardy seeds and cuttings and grow some of the tenderer plants that will not grow outside.

The greenhouse can be both productive and decorative if time and space allow. Climbers such as

Grape vines, Jasmine, Abutilon and the exotic Lapageria can be grown in a narrow border filled with good loamy soil.

On pages 40–41 keep a record of plants you grow in your greenhouse and their progress.

The following are some of the plants which will grow in cool greenhouse conditions. They are also very suitable for conservatories or glazed extensions, provided the winter temperature does not drop below 7°C (45°F).

Bulbs and tubers: Lily, Tigridia, Hippeastrum, Begonia, Gloxinia, Schizanthus, Cyclamen.

Shrubs and perennials: Fuchsia, Pelargonium, Azalea, Polyanthus, Datura, Camellia, Impatiens.

Climbers: Abutilon megapotanicum, Jasminum polyanthus, Lapageria rosea, Plumbago capensis, Solanum jasminoides.

Vegetables and fruit: tomatoes, cucumbers, capsicum, aubergine, melon, grape.

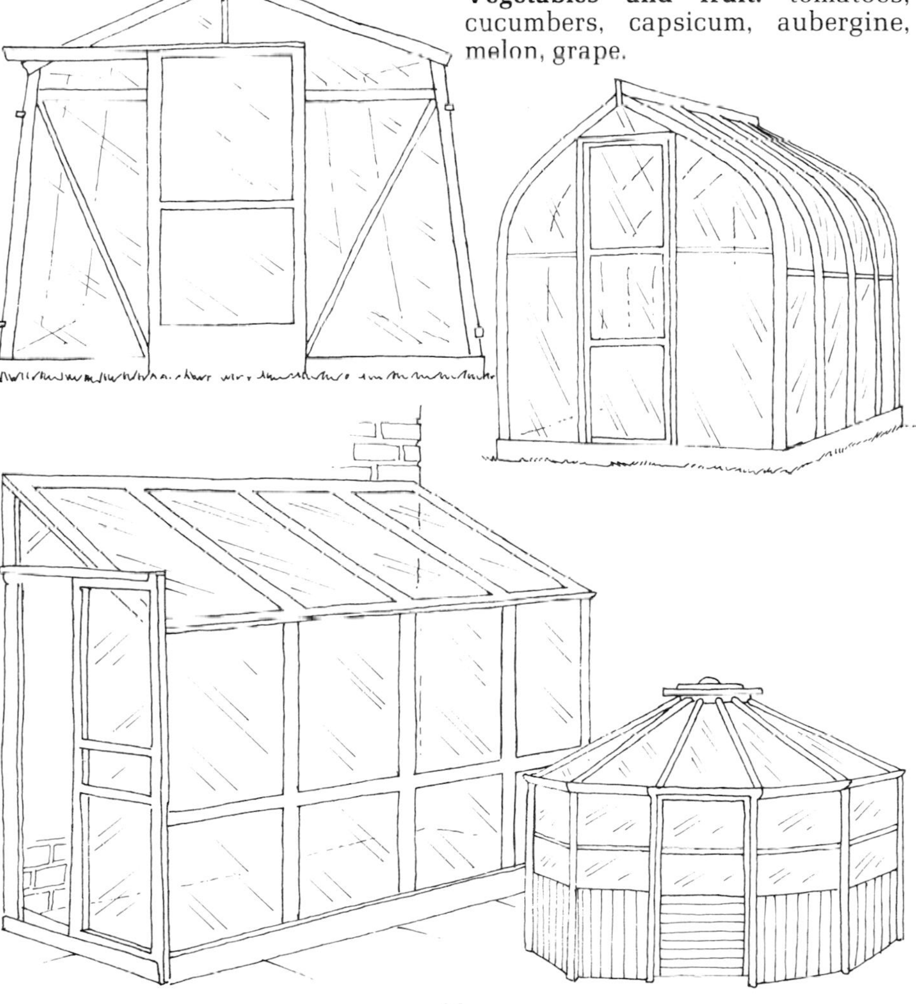

Greenhouse Sowing Chart

Name	Date of Sowing	Results

Name	Date of Sowing	Results

PLANT GUIDE

The following pages offer a small selection of the many plants which are available from nurseries, garden centres and through seed catalogues. It is not intended as a comprehensive list, but rather as an introduction to some of the best.

The majority of these will be available from local garden centres, but there are some, less common, which may have to be ordered. Garden centres offer a wide range of container-grown plants all year round, but do visit some of the larger, specialist nurseries which stock a selection of the less obvious plants.

Finding out about the plants before buying them will save you money and disappointment. A good catalogue can be a really useful source of advice about which varieties are best, and how and where to grow them. Garden centres can be a source of great temptation, but be sure that the plant is suitable for your requirements: how big will it grow, does it look interesting when not in flower? Don't always be tempted into buying shrubs in flower – better to choose those with plenty of young, healthy growth. A shrub in flower has reached maturity and will not grow as vigorously afterwards.

Most plants are pretty long-suffering and will put up with amazingly adverse conditions, but if you give them a good soil, sun or shade according to their needs, keep them free of weeds and water well in dry spells and when they are first planted, they should flourish. Where heights are given in the charts they are guides to the approximate eventual height a plant *may* attain.

Annuals and Biennials

Annuals and biennials will fill the summer garden and patio with bold and brilliant blocks of colour. They are invaluable for quick effect, and help solve the problem of weed invasion in newly planted beds while the slower-growing plants are establishing themselves. The following is a list of the many easily grown from seed. Annuals flower the year they are planted, biennials the following year. Follow instructions on the seed packet for sowing depth.

H.A. = **hardy annual,** H.B. = **hardy biennial**
p. shade = **partial shade**
Height: 1 = **to 20 cm (8 inch),** 2 = **20–45 cm (8–18 inches)**
3 = **45–60 cm (18–24 inches),** 4 = **over 60 cm (24 inches)**

Name	Sow	Flowers	Colour	Height	Aspect
Calendula H.A. (Marigold)	Mar-May	May-Aug	orange yellow	2	sun p.shade
Centaurea H.A.	Mar-Apr	Jun-Sep	blue mixed	2,4	sun p.shade
Cheiranthus H.B. (Wallflower)	Jun	May-Jun	orange yellow	2	sun p.shade
Clarkia H.A.	Mar-Apr	Jul-Aug	red, pink mixed	3	sun
Cosmos H.A.	Apr-May	Jul-Sep	red, orange mixed	3,4	sun p.shade
Delphinium H.A.	Sep	Jun-Sep	pink, blue white	2,4	sun p.shade
Digitalis H.B. (Foxglove)	Jul	Jun-Jul	pink white	4	p.shade
Dimorphotheca H.A. (Cape Marigold)	Apr-May	Jul-Sep	orange mixed	2	sun
Echium H.A.	Mar-Apr	Jul-Aug	blue mixed	2	sun p.shade

Name	Sow	Flowers	Colour	Height	Aspect
Eschscholzia H.A.	Mar-Apr	Jun-Aug	mixed	2	sun
Godetia H.A.	Mar-Apr	Jun-Aug	mixed	2,4	sun p.shade
Iberis H.A. (Candytuft)	Mar-May	May-Sep	pink, white mixed	1,2	sun
Lavatera H.A. (Mallow)	Apr	Jul-Sep	pink white	4	sun p.shade
Linum H.A. (Flax)	Mar-Apr	Jul-Aug	red white	4	sun p.shade
Matthiola H.A. (Stock)	Apr	Jun-Sep	mixed	2,3	sun
Myosotis H.B. (Forget-me-not)	Jun-Jul	Apr-May	blue pink	1,2	sun p.shade
Nemesia H.A.	May	Jul-Sep	blue, red mixed	1	sun p.shade
Nigella H.A. (Love-in-a-Mist)	Mar-Apr	May-Aug	blue, pink white	2,3	sun p.shade
Papaver H.A. (Poppy)	Mar-Apr	Jun-Sep	mixed	3,4	sun p.shade
Phlox H.A.	Mar-Apr	Jul-Oct	mixed	1,2	sun p.shade
Tagetes H.A. (French Marigold)	Apr-May	Jul-Oct	gold yellow	1,2	sun
Tropaeolum majus H.A. (Nasturtium)	Apr-May	Jul-Sep	red, orange mixed	2	sun p.shade

Annuals and Biennials

Name	Date of Sowing	Results

Name	Date of Sowing	Results

Bulbs

Bulbs take up little space and will give colour in the garden almost all year round. Most appreciate a well-cultivated soil and look better planted in clumps or drifts. Allow the leaves of narcissi to die back naturally so as to encourage healthy growth and flowering the following year.

M = **Moisture loving** W.D. = **Well-drained soil**

Name and Height	Plant	Flowers	Colour	Comments
Amaryllis belladonna 60 cm (24 inches)	Jul-Aug	Aug-Oct	white pink	M. W.D. Best on warm south wall
Chionodoxa 15 cm (6 inches)	Oct	Feb-Mar	blue	W.D. Full sun
Colchicum autumnale (Autumn Crocus) 15 cm (6 inches)	Jul	Sep	lilac white	Full sun
Crinum powellii 45 cm (18 inches)	May	Jul-Sep	pink white	Full sun, shelter
Crocus 10 cm (4 inches)	Sept-Oct	Jan-Apr	white purple yellow	W.D. Full sun
Cyclamen neapolitanum 10 cm (4 inches)	Sep-Oct	Aug-Nov	rose pink	Partial or full shade. Good under trees
Eranthis hyemalis (Winter Aconite) 5 cm (2 inches)	Aug-Sep	Jan-Feb	yellow	M. Partial shade
Erythronium (Dogs-tooth Violet) 15 cm (6 inches)	Sep	Mar-Apr	violet purple	M. Partial shade
Fritillaria meleagris 30 cm (12 inches)	Sep-Nov	Apr-Jun	purple green	M. Best in rough grass

Name and Height	Plant	Flowers	Colour	Comments
Galanthus nivalis (Snowdrop) 15 cm (6 inches)	Jul-Aug	Jan	white	In grass or among shrubs
Hyacinth 15–30 cm (6–12 inches)	Oct	Mar-Apr	blue, pink white	W.D. Full sun
Leucojum (Snowflake) 45 cm (18 inches)	Oct	Apr-May	white and green	M. Partial shade
Muscari (Grape Hyacinth) 20 cm (8 inches)	Sep-Oct	Mar-May	blue	Full sun
Narcissus (Daffodil) to 45 cm (18 inches)	Sep	Jan on	white to yellow	Full sun. Many varieties
Ornithogalum 45 cm (18 inches)	Mar-Apr	Jun	white	Sun or partial shade
Scilla 15 cm (6 inches)	Oct	May-Jun	blue	M. W.D. Partial shade
Tulip 30–45 cm (12–18 inches)	Nov	Apr-Jun	various	W.D. Full sun. Many varieties

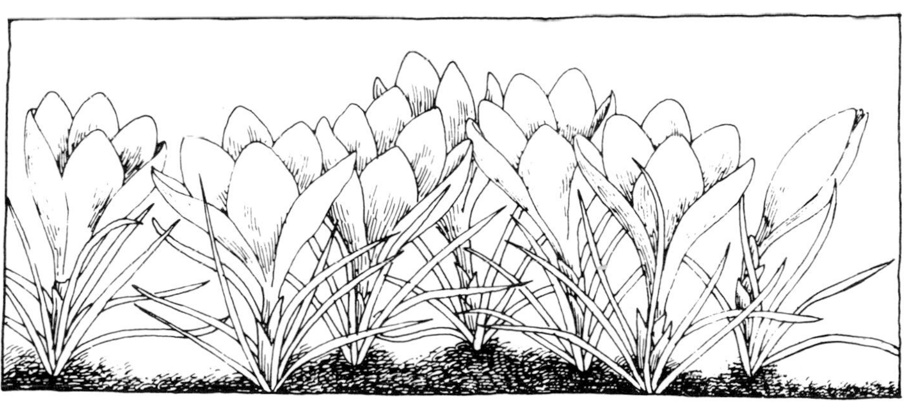

Bulbs

Name	Where Planted	Comments

Name	Where Planted	Comments

Hardy Border Plants

These are mainly herbaceous plants which 'perform' between April and October, die back in the winter and reappear the following spring. A few have evergreen leaves. Dead heading spent flowers will encourage new buds. Stake the taller varieties.

p.shade = **partial shade** f.shade = **full shade**
E = **evergreen** G.C. = **suitable for ground cover**

Name and Height	Flowers	Colour	Aspect	Comments
Achillea 'Moonshine' 60 cm (24 inches)	Jun-Aug	pale yellow	full sun	Silvery foliage
Ajuga reptans E 'Burgundy Glow' 15 cm (6 inches)	May-Jun	blue	sun p.shade	G.C. Bronze leaf
Alchemilla mollis 45 cm (18 inches)	Jun-Jul	green-yellow	sun p.shade	G.C. Pretty leaf
Alstroemeria Ligtu hybrids 60 cm (24 inches)	Jun	pink and orange	full sun	Rich soil
Anemone x hybrida 'September Charm' 60 cm (24 inches)	Aug-Oct	soft pink	sun p.shade f.shade	Late-flowering
Aquilegia McKana hybrids 60 cm (24 inches)	May-Jun	mixed	sun p.shade	Needs moisture
Brunnera macrophylla 45 cm (18 inches)	May-Jun	blue	sun p.shade f.shade	G.C.
Campanula persicifolia 'Telham Beauty' To 90 cm (36 inches)	Jun-Aug	blue	sun p.shade	Needs moisture

Name and Height	Flowers	Colour	Aspect	Comments
Convallaria E (Lily-of-the-Valley) 20 cm (8 inches)	Apr-May	white	p.shade	G.C. Fragrant Needs moisture
Coreopsis verticillata 60 cm (24 inches)	Jun-Sep	yellow	sun	Good for cutting
Crocosmia masonorum 75 cm (30 inches)	Jul-Aug	flame	full sun	Lovely by paths or front of border
Dianthus E 'White Ladies' 30 cm (12 inches)	Jun-Jul	white	sun	Well-drained soil
Dicentra spectabilis 'Bleeding Heart' 75 cm (30 inches)	Jun	rose pink	sun p.shade	Unusual flower. Good foliage. Moist soil
Epimedium perralderianum 30 cm (12 inches)	Apr-May	yellow	p.shade f.shade	G.C. Cool moist soil
Euphorbia polychroma 45 cm (18 inches)	Apr-May	greeny-yellow	sun p.shade	Mound-forming
Geranium grandiflorum alpinum 30 cm (12 inches)	May-Jun	blue	sun p.shade	G.C. Easy
Geum 'Fire Opal' 75 cm (30 inches)	Jun-Sep	orange	sun	Rich soil
Heleborus niger (Christmas Rose) 30 cm (12 inches)	Jan-Mar	white	p.shade f.shade	Moist rich loam. Feed with manure in spring
Hemerocallis (Day Lily) 45 cm (18 inches)	Jun-Aug	various	sun p.shade	Moist soil. Plant in clumps

Hardy Border Plants

Name and Height	Flowers	Colour	Aspect	Comments
Hosta sieboldiana 75 cm (30 inches)	Jul-Aug	lilac	p.shade	Huge, striking leaf. Protect against snails
Kniphofia galpinii (Red Hot Poker) 45 cm (18 inches)	Sep-Oct	orange	sun	Well-drained soil. Moisture. Smaller than some
Lamium maculatum E 'Chequers' 30 cm (12 inches)	May	pink	p.shade f.shade	Marbled leaf. G.C. Good under trees
Paeonia 'Lady Alexander Duff' 75 cm (30 inches)	Jun	pale pink	sun	Deep rich soil. Leave undisturbed
Phlox panniculata 60 cm (24 inches)	Jun	mixed	p.shade	Light moist soil. Feed in May
Pyrethrum 'Eileen May Robinson' 60 cm (24 inches)	May-Aug	pink	sun	Light soil. Feed with compost
Solidago 'Loddon Gold' (Golden Rod) 1 m (3 feet)	Sep-Oct	yellow	sun p.shade	Good back of border
Stachys lanata E 30 cm (12 inches)	Jun-Aug	magenta	sun shade	G.C. Silver felty leaf
Verbascum 'Gainsborough' 1.2 m (4 feet)	Jul-Aug	primrose yellow	sun	Good on chalk. Very striking. Felty leaves
Vinca minor E 'Bowles variety' 7.5 cm (3 inches)	Jul-Oct	blue	p.shade f.shade	G.C. Useful under trees. Trim in spring
Viola hederacea 7.5 cm (3 inches)	May-Jul	violet	p.shade f.shade	G.C. Good in shady corners

Name	Where Planted	Comments

Hardy Border Plants

Name	Where Planted	Comments

Name	Where Planted	Comments

Shrubs

Unless otherwise indicated, all these shrubs will grow in ordinary garden soil. Camellias and Azaleas grown in limy soils can be given an occasional watering with Sequestrene if they show signs of chlorosis (yellowing leaves).

E = **Evergreen** L.H. = **Lime-hating** W.D. = **Well-drained soil**
p.shade = **partial shade** f.shade = **full shade**

Name and Height	Flowers	Colour	Aspect	Comments
Arundinaria nitida E (Bamboo) to 3 m (9 feet)			p.shade	L.H. Needs shelter and moisture. Clump forming. Fast
Azalea kurume E 'Hino-mayo' 45 cm (18 inches)	Apr	pink	p.shade	L.H. Needs shelter. Neat form
Berberis thunbergii 'Atropurpurea' to 1.2 m (4 feet)	May-Jun	yellow	sun	Bronze-purple leaf. Autumn colour
Camellia japonica E 'Donation' to 1.2 m (4 feet)	Feb-Mar	pink	p.shade	L.H. W.D. Shelter. Many other colours. Good pot shrub
Ceanothus E 'Cascade' to 2.5 m (8 feet)	May-Jun	blue	sun	Best againt sunny wall. Shelter. Spreading shape
Chaenomeles speciosa 'Simonii' 60 cm (24 inches)	Feb-Mar	dark red	sun p.shade	Best against low wall or on bank. Spreading shape
Choisya ternata E (Mexican Orange Blossom) to 3 m (6 feet)	May	white	sun p.shade	Fragrant. Shelter. Good dense screen
Cistus x purpureus E (Rock Rose) 1.2 m (4 feet)	May-Jul	deep rose	sun	Poor dry soil. Shelter. Dense growth. Free-flowering

Name and Height	Flowers	Colour	Aspect	Comments
Cornus alba 'Elegantissima' 1.5 m (5 feet) plus			p.shade f.shade	Moist soil. Silver and green leaf. Red stems in winter
Corylopsis pauciflora 1.5 m (5 feet)	Feb-Mar	primrose yellow	p.shade	L.H. Shelter
Cotoneaster horizontalis E to 1 m (3 feet)			p.shade f.shade	Fan-shape hugs wall. Scarlet berries in the autumn
Cytisus battandieri (Moroccan Broom) to 2.5 m (8 feet)	Jun	golden yellow	sun	Dry light soil. Wall shrub. Silvery leaf
Cytisus praecox (Broom) 1.2 m (4 feet)	May	creamy yellow	sun	Dry light soil. Clip back after flowering
Elaeagnus pungens E 'Aureo-variegata' 1.5 m (5 feet)			sun p.shade	Gold and green leaf. Slow and spreading
Fuchsia magellanica 'Alba' to 1.5 m (5 feet)	Jul-Oct	palest pink	sun p.shade	Shelter. Wall shrub
Hamamelis mollis (Witch Hazel) 2 m (6 feet)	Dec-Mar	soft yellow	sun p.shade	L.H. Shelter. Upright growth
Hebe 'Great Orme' 60 cm (24 inches)	Jul-Oct	pink	sun p.shade	W.D. Shelter from frosts. Upright growth
Hypericum patulum 'Hidcote' 1 m (3 feet)	Jun-Oct	yellow	sun p.shade	Tolerates poor soil
Indigofera gerardiana 1 m (3 feet)	Jun-Oct	rose purple	sun	W.D. light soil. Tender. Wall shelter. Arching shape

Shrubs

Name and Height	Flowers	Colour	Aspect	Comments
Kerria japonica 1.5 m (5 feet)	Apr-May	yellow	p.shade f.shade	Any soil. Easy. Single rather than usual double flower
Kolkwitzia amabilis 'Pink Cloud' 1.5 m (5 feet)	May-Jun	pink	sun p.shade	Broad and twiggy. Free-flowering
Lavandula spica E 'Hidcote' 30 cm (12 inches)	Jul-Sep	deep purple	sun	W.D. light soil. Trim April and August
Magnolia stellata 1 m (3 feet)	Mar-Apr	white	sun	Shelter, Smaller than other Magnolias. Free-flowering. Slow
Mahonia japonica E to 1.5 m (5 feet)	Jan-Mar	yellow	p.shade f.shade	Needs space. Best at back of border
Philadelphus 'Sybille' 1.2 m (4 feet)	Jun-Jul	white	sun p.shade	Fragrant. Prune out spent flowering shoots July
Pieris E 'Forest Flame' to 1.5 m (5 feet)	May	white	p.shade f.shade	L.H. Shelter. Grown for striking red-pink of young leaf
Potentilla 'Tangerine' 60 cm (24 inches)	May-Nov	soft orange	sun p.shade	Easy. Many varieties. This produces best colour in light shade
Pyracantha rogersiana E to 2.2 m (7 feet)	Jun	cream	sun p.shade f.shade	Good for dark walls. Scarlet berries. Spreading

Name and Height	Flowers	Colour	Aspect	Comments
Ribes sanguineum 'Pulborough Scarlet' 2 m (6 feet)	Apr-May	deep red	p.shade f.shade	Upright. Fast. Good for quick effect
Ruta graveolens E 'Jackman's Blue' 60 cm (24 inches)	Jul	yellow	sun p.shade	Dense rounded shape. Blue-grey leaf. Clip to keep shape
Senecio laxifolius E 1 m (3 feet)	Jun	yellow	sun	Silver-grey leaves. Spreading. Prune in spring
Spiraea thunbergii 1 m (3 feet)	Mar-Apr	white	sun p.shade	Small and twiggy. Easy. Free-flowering
Viburnum fragrans 2 m (6 feet)	Nov-Feb	pale pink	sun p.shade	Slender upright growth. Intermittent winter flowering

Shrubs

Name	Where Planted	Comments

Name	Where Planted	Comments

Trees

The average garden doesn't have room for large numbers of trees, so making a choice of one or two out of hundreds can be hard. The best advice is to choose a tree which can be a feature in all seasons. The choice here has been limited to those which are suitable for small gardens and have year-round interest.

Name	Height	Flowers	Colour	Comments
Acer palmatum 'atropurpureum' (Japanese Maple)	to 1.5 m (5 feet)		Brilliant red foliage	Striking specimen. Very slow and spreading
Crataegus oxycantha 'Paul's Scarlet' (Hawthorn)	4–5 m (12–15 feet)	May	crimson	Neat upright shape. Attractive berries
Laburnum vossii	4 m (12 feet)	Jun	golden	Small upright and arching. Poisonous seeds
Malus 'floribunda' (Crab Apple)	3–4 m (9–12 feet)	Apr	pink	Slender, arching shape. Very free-flowering
Prunus 'Tai Haku' (Flowering Cherry)	5 m (15 feet)	Apr	white	Beautiful, spreading shape. Young leaves red
Pyrus salicifolia 'pendula' (Weeping Pear)	4–5 m (12–15 feet)	Apr	white	Weeping shape. Lovely specimen tree. Silver 'willow' leaves
Robinia pseudoacacia 'Frisia'	to 6 m (18 feet)			Light airy tree. Delicate golden-yellow foliage
Sorbus aucuparia 'vilmorinii' (Mountain Ash)	to 6 m (18 feet)			Delicate arching shape. Graceful fern-like leaves. Orange berries

Name	Where Planted	Comments

Climbers

All climbers need some kind of vertical support but vary in their methods of extending themselves. The few self-clingers, like ivy and Virginia creeper, will adhere or hook themselves onto surfaces and do not need tying in. The rest, twiners and ramblers, need wires or trellis to guide and support the shoots. The general rule with Clematis is to keep their roots in the shade and their heads in the sun. Climbing roses are listed in the section on roses.

p.shade = **partial shade** f.shade = **full shade**

Name and Height	Flowers	Colour	Aspect	Comments
Actinidia kolomikta to 4 m (12 feet)			sun p.shade	Heart-shaped leaves, cream and pink. May be slow to establish
Campsis grandiflora 3 m (9 feet)	Aug	orange scarlet	sun	Not fully hardy. Warm sheltered wall. Large trumpet flowers
Clematis 'Perle d'Azur' 3–5 m (9–15 feet)	Jun-Oct	sky blue	sun p.shade	Prune hard to 60 cm (24 inches) of base in Feb
Clematis jackmanii 'Superba' 4–9 m (12–27 feet)	Jun-Sep	deep purple	sun p.shade	Prune as above
Clematis montana 'Elizabeth' 7–10 m (21–30 feet)	May-Jun	soft pink	sun p.shade	Prune in June only if necessary. Well-drained soil
Hedera helix E 'Goldheart' 2–3 m (6–9 feet)			p.shade f.shade	Self-clinging. Small leaf, gold centre
Hydrangea petiolaris (Climbing Hydrangea) 2–3 m (6–9 feet)	Jun-Jul	white	p.shade f.shade	Self-clinging
Jasminum nudiflorum E (Winter Jasmine) to 3 m (9 feet)	Nov-Mar	yellow	sun p.shade	Arching growth; needs tying to support

Name and Height	Flowers	Colour	Aspect	Comments
Jasminum officinale (Summer Jasmine) 5–7 m (15–21 feet)	Jun-Sep	white	sun p.shade	Fragrant
Lonicera japonica 'Halliana' 8–10 m (24–30 feet)	Jun-Sep	creamy yellow	p.shade f.shade	Fragrant. Needs moisture. Semi-evergreen
Parthenocissus Henryana (Virginia Creeper) to 5 m (15 feet)			p.shade f.shade	Shorter and slower than the usual, but finer leaf and autumn colour
Passiflora coerulea (Passion Flower) 4 m (12 feet)	Jun-Sep	white and blue	sun p.shade	Fragrant. Curious flower, orange fruit. Prune in March
Solanum crispum (Chilean Potato-tree) 3 m (9 feet)	Jul-Oct	mauve	sun	Needs sheltered sunny wall. Herbaceous stems
Vitis coignetiae (Glory Vine) 8–10 m (24–30 feet)			sun p.shade	Huge leaves; brilliant autumn colour when not in shade
Wisteria sinensis 8–10 m (24–30 feet)	May-Jun	mauve	sun	May be slow to flower

Climbers

Name	Where Planted	Comments

Name	Where Planted	Comments

Roses

Bush and shrub roses
The modern bush roses are colourful, reliable, long-flowering and neat in growth, which makes them very suitable for small areas. The larger old shrub and species roses demand space, are less reliable and more prone to disease. But they include some of the most beautiful roses of all, with muted colours and informal habit. The Modern Shrub roses combine the qualities of both. These are a few of the best of old and new. The flowering season lasts from approximately June to October. For notes on soil, position, etc. see August, 'Gardener's Year'.

Climbing and rambler roses
Ramblers have long flexible canes which will ramble over walls, sheds, trellis, pergolas, even into trees.
Climbers are shorter-growing with the angular kind of growth more typical of bush and shrub roses from which they are derived. Best grown on walls.

BUSH ROSES

Name	Colour	Height	Comments
All Gold (Floribunda)	yellow	60 cm (24 in)	Small double flower, glossy foliage. Wide-branching growth
Dearest (Floribunda)	salmon pink	75 cm (30 in)	Fragrant, free-flowering. Bushy growth
Iceberg (Floribunda)	white	1.8 m (5 feet)	Large, open flower. Vigorous and leafy. Free-flowering
Lilli Marlene (Floribunda)	crimson red	75 cm (30 in)	Large semi-double flowers in clusters. Neat and upright
Josephine Bruce (Hybrid Tea)	dark crimson	1 m (3 feet)	Fragrant. Double, dark velvet flower. Leafy and sturdy
Wendy Cussons (Hybrid Tea)	rosy red	1 m (3 feet)	Fragrant; full flower. Vigorous and free-flowering

OLD AND MODERN SHRUB ROSES

Name	Colour	Height	Comments
Cecile Brunner (China Rose)	shell pink	60 cm (24 in)	Tiny shapely flowers. Delicate form. Free-flowering
Fantin Latour ('Cabbage' Rose)	pale pink	1.8 m (5½ feet)	Lovely double flower. Wide growth. Free-flowering
Frühlingsmorgen (Modern Shrub)	pink gold	1.8 m (5½ feet)	Single open flowers. Long arching stems. Repeat flowering
Golden Wings (Modern Shrub)	pale yellow	1.8 m (5½ feet)	Fragrant. Single flower. Graceful and spreading
Madame Hardy (Damask Rose)	white	1.5 m (5 feet)	Perfect double flower, green centre. Vigorous and leafy
Mme Pierre Oger (Bourbon Rose)	shell pink	1.5 m (5 feet)	Cup-shaped double flower. Neat, upright shape
Nevada (Modern Shrub)	creamy white	to 2 m (6 feet)	Lovely open flower. Wide-arching shape. One of the finest
Tuscany Superb (Gallica)	crimson purple	1.5 m (5 feet)	Double, deep velvet flowers. Wide arching form
Xanthina 'Canary Bird' (Species)	clear yellow	to 2 m (6 feet)	Single flower. Slender arching branches. Beautiful 'wild' rose

Roses

CLIMBING AND RAMBLER ROSES

Name	Colour	Height	Comments
Alberic Barbier (Rambler)	creamy white	to 7 m (21 feet)	Fragrant double flowers. Dark foliage. Good screen
Albertine (Rambler)	copper pink	to 7 m (21 feet)	Clusters of loose double flowers. Very vigorous
Danse du Feu (Perpetual Climber)	vivid red	3 m (9 feet)	Large double flower. Free-flowering
Etoile de Hollande (Climber)	dark red	to 6 m (18 feet)	Fragrant. Will grow on north or east wall
Gloire de Dijon (Climber)	buff yellow	to 5 m (15 feet)	Fragrant, free-flowering old rose
Golden Showers (Perpetual Climber)	gold yellow	2.8 m (8 feet)	Short climber. Flowers all summer
Mme Alfred Carrière (Climber)	white	to 5 m (15 feet)	Small shapely flower. Free-flowering, even on a north wall

Name	Where Planted	Comments

Rock-Garden Plants

Some small, low-growing shrubs and shrubby perennials suitable for rock gardens and dry sunny banks. Need full sun and a limy, sharply drained soil. Give *Erica carnea* some peat.

Name	Flowers	Colour	Height	Comments
Campanula Many varieties; trailing or upright	Jun-Aug	blue mauve white	5–20 cm (2–8 in)	Trailing kinds grow in dry stone walls
Dianthus E Miniature rock Pinks; many varieties	Jun	pink white	5–15 cm (2–6 in)	Crevices and walls
Erica carnea E Low trailing Heathers; many varieties	Nov-Apr	white red pink	15–30 cm (6–12 in)	Trim after flowering. More lime-tolerant than other varieties
Geranium Many varieties	Jun	pink blue	5–15 cm (2–6 in)	Easy and colourful
Helianthemum E Shrubby Sunroses; many varieties	May-Jul	orange pink yellow	15–30 cm (6–12 in)	Some grey-leaved. Trim after flowering
Phlox subulata Many varieties	May-Jun	pink red	15 cm (6 in)	Trailing and bushy
Saxifraga E Many varieties	Apr-Jun	white pink	5–20 cm (2–8 in)	Rosette leaves or 'pin cushions'
Veronica E Rock Speedwell; many varieties	Jun	blue	5–15 cm (2–6 in)	Neat and bushy

Name	Where Planted	Comments

Water Garden Plants

Plants for the water garden, equally suitable for moist shady corners. Most grow on the margins, a few will stand in shallow water. The leaf is often as, if not more, attractive than the flower.

Name	Flowers	Colour	Height	Comments
Astilbe Many varieties	Jun-Aug	pink red	45–90 cm (18–36 in)	Attractive leaf and flower
Caltha palustris Marsh Marigold	Mar-May	yellow	30–45 cm (12–18 in)	Damp edge or shallow water
Ferns Many varieties			30–120 cm (12–48 in)	
Filipendula ulmaria 'Aurea'			30–45 cm (12–18 in)	Golden leaf Apr-Oct. Stop flower
Hosta Many varieties	Jul-Aug	lilac	30–75 cm (12–30 in)	Grow for foliage; variegated types
Iris laevigata Other varieties	Jul-Aug	blue white	60 cm (24 in)	Will grow in shallow water
Mimulus luteus	Jun-Sep	gold yellow	30 cm (12 in)	Brightly coloured. Shallow water
Primula florindae Other varieties	Jun-Jul	yellow	75 cm (30 in)	Try also 'Candelabra' Primulas

Name	Where Planted	Comments

Fruit

All fruit does best in full sun, on a medium loam soil. Good drainage is important and the addition of some mortar rubble when digging and fertilizing will help. Topdress with manure and a fruit fertilizer. Correct pruning and regular spraying against pests and disease are vital to good fruit production.

In the case of apples and pears, find out whether the varieties you have chosen fruit on new or old wood, as this affects which part to cut. Redcurrant fruits on new wood, blackcurrant on old.

Summer-pruning applies to fruit grown as cordons, pyramids or fans. As a general rule, cut back side shoots to within 5 buds of the main stem.

Sweet Cherry is not economical for small gardens, since it is self-sterile and not available in dwarf forms. Morello Cherry (Sour Cherry) will grow on north walls.

Strawberry requires a lot of space to make a worthwhile crop; best grown in the vegetable patch if you have one. Protect with netting against birds. Propagate by layering, that is peg down the healthiest runners until they have rooted, sever and transplant (see June, 'Gardener's Year'). Discard the parent plant after 3 years. Save space by growing strawberries in a special pot.

S = **standard** H-S = **half standard**
B = **bush** P = **pyramid** C = **cordon**
F = **fan**

Name	Fruits	Forms	Pruning Times
Apple Dessert and cookers in variety	Aug-Oct	S, H–S, B, P, C, F	Winter-prune: Dec-Mar Summer-prune: Jul, restricted forms
Blackberry	Jul-Sep	Canes	Cut back: Oct
Blackcurrant	Jul-Aug	B	Prune back to strong new shoots after fruiting: Aug
Cherry, Morello (Cooking)	Jul-Aug	B, F	Summer-prune: May, restricted forms. No other pruning
Gooseberry	Jun-Aug	B, C	Winter-prune: Dec-Mar Summer-prune, cordons: Jul
Peach and Nectarine	Jul-Aug	B, F	Summer-prune: May, restricted forms. No other pruning

Name	Fruits	Forms	Pruning Times
Pear Dessert and cookers in variety	Aug-Oct	S, H–S, B, P, C, F	Winter-prune: Dec-Mar Summer-prune: Jul, restricted forms
Plums and Gages In variety	Jul-Sep	S, H–S, B, P, C, F	Summer-prune: May, restricted forms. No other pruning
Raspberry and Loganberry	Jul-Sep	Canes	Shorten tips: Feb. Cut back: Aug
Redcurrant	Jul	B, C, F	Winter-prune: Dec-Mar Summer-prune: Jun, restricted forms

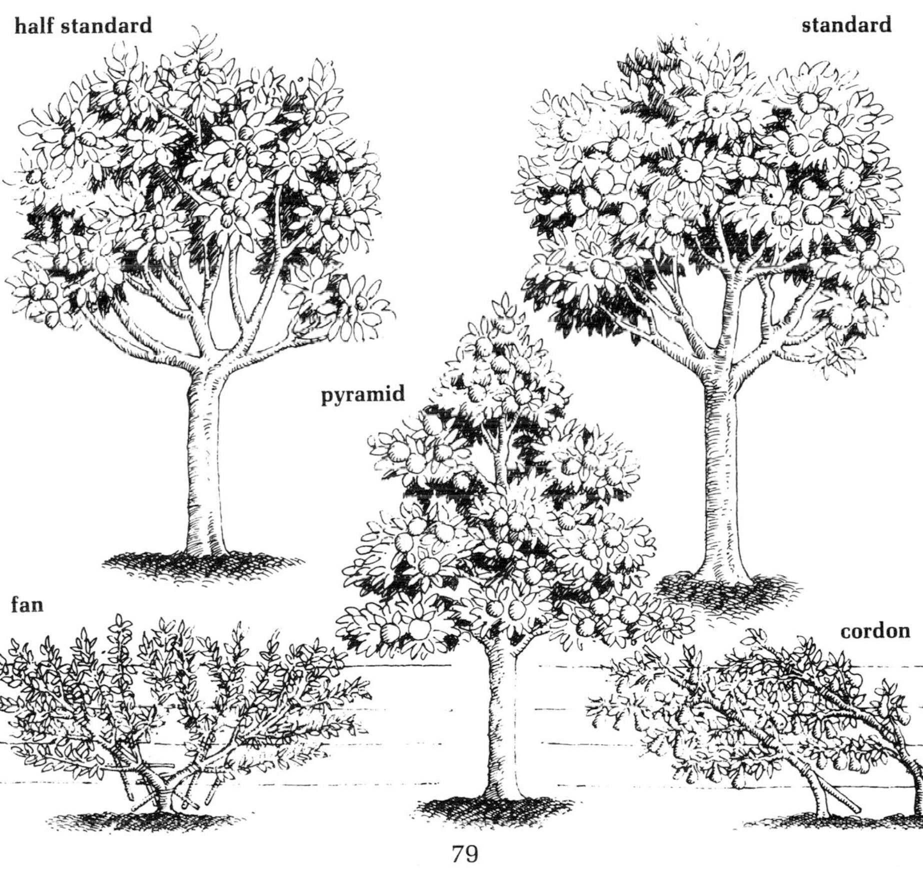

Fruit

Name	Crop	Pruning

Name	Crop	Pruning

Vegetables

Vegetables need a well-cultivated soil, dug and manured at depth, and a place in full sun. Regular watering, weeding and pest control are essential. This is a small selection of vegetables and salads which are easily grown and take up relatively little space, plus a few which provide a good, continuous supply of nutritious greenery in the winter months and spring.

Name and When to Sow	Plant or Transplant	Harvest	Pests and Diseases	Comments
Beans, Broad Jan-Apr in succession		May on	blackfly	Harvest before pods toughen. Early sowings under cloches
Beans, French May-Jul		Jul-Oct according to variety	aphids	Need warmth
Beans, Runner May-Jun		Jul-Sep	blackfly	Rich soil. Mulch and water well
Beetroot Apr-May in succession		Jul on	blackfly	Harvest while small
Calabrese Apr-Jul in succession		Jul-Oct	caterpillar cabbage root fly	Stopped by frosts
Carrot Early: Mar-Jun Late: May-Jul in succession		Jun-Jul Aug-Nov	carrot fly	Light, rich soil
Lettuce Mar-Aug in succession		Jun-Oct according to variety	aphids slugs snails	Rich soil. Water well

Name and When to Sow	Plant or Transplant	Harvest	Pests and Diseases	Comments
Onion Mar-Apr	sets Feb-Apr	Aug on	onion fly mildew	Light, rich soil. Lift, dry and store
Peas Mar-Jun in succession		as ready		Rich soil. Light shade
Potato, Early	seed potato Mar-Apr	late Jun on	less prone than later varieties	Earth up tubers when 23 cm (9 inches) high
Radish Mar-Jul in succession		Apr-Sep		Light, rich soil
Shallot	sets Dec-Mar	Jun		Lift, dry and store
Spinach, Summer Mar-Jun in succession		May-Sep	aphids mildew	Small successional sowings
Spinach, Beet Perpetual Apr on		Aug on	aphids	Second sowing in July for later crop
Tomato	Jun-Apr	Late Aug-Sep		Stop plant 2 leaves above 4th flower truss

Vegetables

Name	Date of Sowing	Results

Name	Date of Sowing	Results

Herbs

Herbs grown for culinary purposes may be annuals, biennials, perennials or small shrubs. Only Bay is likely to grow to any great height. It is usually the leaf, sometimes the seed, which is harvested and used. With the exception of mint, all do best in full sun and most prefer a light, well-drained soil. Basil and Sweet Marjoram are unlikely to survive the winter in this country and are therefore best treated as annuals and resown each year. The following can easily be grown from seed.

Name	Sow	Harvest	Comments
Basil Half-hardy annual	May	Jul-Sep	Well-drained soil
Chervil Hardy biennial	Mar-Apr	May-Jun	Moist soil
Coriander Hardy annual	Mar-Apr	Jun-Jul	Use seed and leaf
Dill Hardy annual	Mar-Apr	May-Jun	Use seed and leaf
Marjoram, sweet knotted Hardy perennial	Apr	Jun	Full sun
Parsley Hardy biennial	Mar-Apr	Jun	Moist fertile soil. Shelter

Perennial Herbs

Chives (Allium schoenoprasum): *Plant offsets March. Harvest as required. Pick off flower heads to increase leaves. Fertile soil, sun or semi-shade. Divide clumps Sept/Oct every 3 or 4 years.*

Fennel (Foeniculum vulgare): *Plant March. Harvest July. Any well-drained soil. Sun. Decorative plant, growing to 1.5 m (5 feet). Self-seeding. Use leaf and seed. This is not the bulbous type, Florence Fennel.*

Marjoram, pot (Origanum onites): *Plant March. Harvest Jul-Sep. Well-drained soil, full sun.* O. majorana *(sweet knotted marjoram) has a better flavour.*

Mint (Mentha spp): *Plant March. Harvest as required. Moist soil, shady position. Very invasive; restrict by growing in a container in the ground.* Mentha rotundifolia *has the best flavour.*

Tarragon (Artemisia dracunculus): *Plant March. Harvest Jun-Sep. Well-drained, light soil. Full sun. Use leaf. Tends to deteriorate after about 3 seasons.*

Shrubby herbs (Evergreen)

Bay (Laurus nobilis): *May grow to 3 m (9 feet) plus, but can be kept clipped as a bush. Plant Mar-Apr. Sun and shelter. Aromatic leaves – use as required.*

Rosemary (Rosmarinus officinalis): *Grows to about 1 m (3 feet), sometimes more. Plant Mar-Apr. Any soil. Full sun and protection in cold areas. Use leaves as required. Clip back in April, to prevent straggly growth.*

Sage (Salvia officinalis): *May grow to 60 cm (24 inches). Plant Mar-Apr. Well-drained, light soil. Full sun. Use leaves as required. Clip back after flowering. Tends to become straggly and may need replacing after 3–4 years.*

Thyme (Thymus vulgare): *Low-growing or prostrate. Many varieties. Plant Oct-Mar. Well-drained soil. Full sun. Dislikes damp. Trim after flowering to encourage dense growth.*

Herbs

Name	Date of Sowing	Results

Name	Date of Sowing	Results

Pests and Diseases

The healthier your plants and their environment, the less susceptible they will be to the risk of infection. By eliminating the conditions under which pests and diseases flourish, you are halfway to winning the battle. If you still have problems, you may have to use chemicals.

Preventative measures
Take care of the soil by correcting deficiencies and treating such notorious trouble spots as badly-drained areas. Clear regularly all garden debris (in corners, under hedges), destroy weeds, burn or compost waste, wash out pots and containers, keep all tools clean and sharp. When pruning cut cleanly, leaving no ragged edges or open wounds.

Recognize friendly predators – birds, hedgehogs, toads, ladybirds – which will help to keep the pest population down. Pick off visible insects, like greenfly, and don't be squeamish about using your boot on slugs and snails. Greenfly will also succumb to relentless daily sprayings with water.

It is a depressing fact that, having done all this, circumstances beyond your control – particular weather or soil conditions – may still introduce pests and infection into the garden. In that case, you will have to take more drastic action.

If plants look weak or sickly, examine soil, stem, leaf and flower for recognizable pests or tell-tale signs. If you find none, you may have to lift the plant to see if the trouble lies underground in the root system.

Diagnose carefully before rushing out with the spray can. Distinguish between poor growth caused by soil deficiencies and specific infection. The height of the pest season occurs in the spring and summer months. Fungal diseases are often more difficult to diagnose and harder to control. Fruit and vegetables are the prime targets for both in the garden. Precautionary spring spraying and winter-washing of fruit trees will help enormously, as will treating seed beds of susceptible plants in the vegetable garden.

Chemical insecticides and fungicides
These must be used with caution. Some are relatively harmless and safe to use; others, including the systemics, are poisonous to humans, pets, benevolent insects, fish, and may taint food crops.

Read labels carefully and follow instructions on how and when to use to the letter, noting advice about harvesting treated food crops. Always store away from children. Only use slug and snail pellets if you can be sure they won't be found by your children and pets.

There are a confusing number of treatments on the market — often the same chemical under several different brand names. The following chart offers alternative treatments in many cases. You won't need all of them; keep only those suitable for general purposes. Resort to systemics and heavier chemicals if all else has failed.

Pests	Where Found	Treatment
Aphids Greenfly, blackfly, etc	Leaf, fruit, stem: apple, brassica, lettuce, pea, rose. Visible. Pinch off	Malathion Bioresmethrin Derris
Beetles Flea, raspberry	Larvae and adult feed on root and leaf: cane fruits, roses, shrubs, vegetables	Derris Bromophos Gamma-HCH
Capsid Bug	Small green bugs tear holes in leaf, puncture fruit: apple, soft fruit, chrysanthemum	Malathion Diazinon Dimethoate (syst)
Caterpillar Codlin moth, cutworm	Feed on foliage, root, seed and stem: apple, strawberry, brassica, herbaceous plants	Derris Bioresmethrin Trichlorphon
Earwig	Ragged holes in leaf and flower: dahlia, chrysanthemum, brassica. In the greenhouse	Trap with straw in upturned pots. Gamma-HCH
Eelworm	Microscopic. Attack bulb and stem: food crops, bulbs and herbaceous plants	No effective cure. Lift and burn plants
Flies Cabbage-root, carrot, onion	Larvae burrow into roots: brassica, peas, lawns, bulbs. Foliage wilts and dies back	Bromophos granules on soil before planting/sowing
Froghopper	'Cuckoo-spit' on leaves and shoots of herbaceous plants and roses. Syringe with water	Derris Malathion
Leafhopper Rose	Suck sap, causes mottling of leaves. Visible on underside of leaf	Derris Malathion
Leatherjacket	Larvae feed on roots of grass in lawns, vegetables, herbaceous plants	Water turf with Gamma-HCH. Deep digging exposes them
Mites Red spider, greenhouse	Microscopic insects cause severe damage to greenhouse plants, soft fruit, apple, bulbs	Malathion, Derris, Diazinon, Dimethoate (syst.)

Pests	Where Found	Treatment
Mites, Big-bud	Serious damage to leaf-buds of blackcurrant, which swell. If untreated may lead to reversion. Destroy badly affected plants	Difficult to treat. Spray with lime-sulphur as flowers open
Sawfly Rose leaf-rolling, apple	Larvae or caterpillars feed on and disfigure fruit and leaf: wavy scar on apples, rose leaf curls up	Gamma-HCH at petal-fall Derris, Malathion
Slugs and snails	Feed on root, bulb, tuber, leaf and flower: strawberry, vegetables, herbaceous plants	Methiocarb or Metaldehyde pellets
Thrips Pea, greenhouse	Tear tiny holes in foliage, leaving silvery appearance: greenhouse, herbaceous plants, peas	Derris Malathion Diazinon
Weevils Apple-blossom, leaf-eating	Larvae and adults eat foliage, fruit and flower bud on fruit trees, particularly apple, peas, beans	Dress vegetable seed-beds with Gamma-HCH, Derris. Spray fruit with Gamma-HCH in spring
Whitefly	Mainly found on leaves of greenhouse plants, especially tomatoes. Also Brassica	Malathion Pyrethrum Bioresmethrin

Fungal Diseases	Where Found	Treatment
Blight Cane, potato, tomato	Dark blotches on leaves and stems of cane fruits. Potato and tomato can be badly affected	Maneb or Bordeaux Mixture. Cut down and burn badly affected plants
Botrytis Grey mould	Caused by damp, cold conditions. Grey fluff on stem, foliage, fruit. Affects fruit, vegetables, greenhouse plants	Pick off affected parts. Spray regularly with Benomyl

Fungal Diseases	Where Found	Treatment
Brown rot	Flower stalks and young shoots apple, soft fruit. Fruit becomes brown and shrivelled on tree. Can lead to canker if untreated	Cut out affected parts. Destroy any wasp nests: they introduce the disease
Canker	Fruit trees, particularly apple. Sunken patch on bark which widens, exposing wood beneath. Spreads up and down	Cut out infected area; paint wound with fungicidal wound paint. Destroy badly affected trees
Damping-off Seedlings, greenhouse	Seedlings collapse and die. Caused by cold, wet soils and overcrowding of seedlings	Water Cheshunt Compound into soil or seed compost before sowing
Leaf-spot Black spot	Black spot on rose leaves. Brown or black patches on leaves of soft fruit	Frequent applications Benomyl
Mildew Downy	Whitish mildew on underside of foliage. Affects vegetables and bedding plants	Difficult to control. Spray with Thiram or Maneb
Mildew Powdery	Powdery mildew coating stem and foliage, later turning brown: apple, soft fruit, pea, rose, bedding plants	Spray with Dinocap or Benomyl regularly
Rust	Rusty-orange pustules on fruit, bedding and herbaceous plants, roses. Caused by a number of different fungi.	Cut out infected parts. Regular treatment with Thiram, Mancozeb or Zineb
Scab	Hard black patches and scabs on twig, fruit, leaf: apple, pear, peach	Spray with Benomyl, Captan or lime-sulphur at bud-burst and fortnightly until July

Plant Health Record

Plant Name	Pest or Disease	Treatment	Results

Plant Name	Pest or Disease	Treatment	Results

THE GARDENER'S YEAR

This is a month-by-month guide to the main tasks throughout the gardening year. Use it flexibly – the weather is an unpredictable factor and some jobs may have to be put off until it is warmer or wetter.

Each month also has notes on a particular gardening operation or technique, not necessarily tied to that month. These are outlines of basic principles: there are volumes written on the subject of pruning, for instance. Your best guide, once you have understood the principle, will be your own observation of how the plant grows and flowers and its state of health.

Don't worry if you don't get round to every task or have 'missed' a few weeks. For lots of people these jobs have to be fitted into the odd Sunday afternoon in the garden.

But if you do nothing else, the main rule must be to observe hygiene in the garden: clear piles of leaves and rubbish where garden pests can breed undisturbed, cut out dead and unhealthy wood on trees and shrubs, keep weeds down, and water regularly and thoroughly in dry hot spells.

January

Usually very cold. A time to plan for the year ahead, think about changes you want to make in the garden and order plants, seeds and bulbs.

Generally
Check drainage in lawns and aerate.

Sow
Early broad beans in the open if mild, or under cloches.

Prune
Rose bushes between now and March. Winter-prune apple, pear, gooseberry and redcurrant.

Pests and diseases
Fruit trees, especially apples, are susceptible to various pests and fungal diseases. Preventative treatment now will pay off later.
Winter-wash with tar-oil, or equivalent, all fruit trees and bushes against aphids.
Spray with lime-sulphur, or equivalent, apples and pears against scab and canker.

Notes

February

Still very cold. Make sure equipment and tools are in good repair and get plant orders in.

Generally
Continue work on roses and fruit trees.
Prepare for spring planting next month.

Sow
Some early parsley seeds if ground not frosted.
Begin sowing in the greenhouse and under glass.

Prune
Late-flowering Clematis, e.g. Jackmanii – prune hard.
Wisteria – prune new side shoots to within 3 buds of old wood.
Early-flowering raspberry canes – shorten tips.
Late-flowering and new canes – cut down to within 15 cm (6 inches) of ground.

Pests and diseases
Spray peach against leaf-curl.

Notes on sowing
Growing from seed: This is a cheap and easy way to grow flowers and vegetables. Hardy plants can be sown directly outdoors; less hardy plants may need the protection of a cloche or be grown indoors in greenhouse conditions.

Sowing outdoors: Most Hardy annuals and vegetables can be sown directly into a permanent bed (in situ) once the soil is warm enough in early spring. Others – most biennials and some vegetables – need to be sown into a 'nursery' bed and transferred later. Sowing under cloches gives protection from frost and gives you an earlier start.

Prepare the seed bed in advance and cultivate the top layer, 7.5 cm (3 inches), to a fine tilth by raking and sieving. Sow the seeds in drills or channels made with a pointed stick or draw hoe. Sow thinly and evenly and cover with a sprinkling of fine soil.

Scatter by hand for more informal sowings of flowers.

Thin out overcrowded seedlings as they come up.

Sowing indoors: This can be done in seed boxes, trays, pots or a special seed propagator (heated or unheated).

Fill clean containers with seed compost such as John Innes or Levingtons, water, then drain thoroughly: soil should be moist, not sodden. Sow evenly and thinly and cover with a fine layer of sifted soil.

Cover with glass if using boxes or other containers or with the propagator cover and then black polythene or brown paper.

When the seedlings start to show, remove the polythene or paper and allow some ventilation through the glass.

After a few days, remove the glass or cover. Water using a spray or fine rose of a watering can.

Move on to separate pots or outside when the seedlings are large enough to handle.

Notes

March

Early spring, but though daytime temperatures may be warmer watch out for sharp night frosts. Protect tender plants with sacking or straw. The beginning of the sowing and planting season.

Generally

Finish digging over new planting areas as soon as the ground thaws. Fork over.

Rake and brush lawns.

Finish pruning roses.

Sow

First of successional sowings: Brussels sprouts, early carrots, leeks, lettuce, peas, early potato, spinach. Hardy annuals: Calendula, Clarkia, Godetia, Lavatera, etc and herbs. Grass seed for new lawns or prepare seed beds for August sowing. Resow bare patches in established lawns.

Plant or transplant

Shrubs and hardy border plants. Tarragon, Fennel, Marjoram, Mint. Divide and replant 3-year old clumps of chives or plant new offsets.

Prune

Late-flowering shrubs (see April).

Topdress and fertilize

Established roses (after pruning), climbers, flowering shrubs, border plants, especially Paeonies and Lily-of-the-Valley, with compost or manure. Apply spring fertilizer to established lawns.

Notes on sowing lawns from seed

Rough dig area intended for lawn, incorporate compost, fertilizer, etc, and leave over winter for March sowing, over summer for August sowing.

Good drainage is essential. Break up compacted areas, leave in small stones. You may have to lay drains on heavy clay soils.

Level carefully by raking and rolling. Prepare seed bed to a fine tilth, remove large stones, level with rake again and roll with a light garden roller.

Sow seed at a rate of 15–25 g ($\frac{1}{2}$–1 oz) per sq metre (yard). Oversowing produces overcrowded, unhealthy seedlings. Rake lightly and roll again to firm soil.

Protect with netting against birds. Keep moist in dry weather.

The first mowing should take place when the grass is about 5 cm (2 inches) high, after about 3 or 4 weeks.

Notes

April

It should be getting warmer. Spring bulbs are out in full display.

Generally
In dry weather keep new plants well watered.
Water and mulch everywhere to keep weeds down.
Start regular lawn mowing.

Sow
Beetroot, broccoli, peas, marrow, perpetual spinach, broad beans, lettuce.
Tomatoes for the greenhouse.

Plant or transplant
Late-flowering hardy border plants.
Container-grown roses.
Evergreen shrubs.
New strawberry plants.
Lift, divide and replant overgrown clumps of Michelmas daisies.

Prune
Early-flowering shrubs after flowering, e.g. Spiraea, Flowering currant (Ribes), Forsythia.
Trim Lavender, Senecio laxifolius to shape. (Cut hard if straggly.)
Trim winter heathers.

Dress and fertilize
Roses with rose fertilizer.
Give roses, newly planted shrubs and border plants a mulch of compost or manure to feed, supply moisture and keep weeds at bay.

Notes on pruning
The main purposes of pruning are: to cut out weak and diseased wood; to encourage new growth, flower and fruit. It may also be used to encourage a shape not natural to the plant, e.g. fruit cordons.

Standard pruning: Cut out any branches which grow inwards and those that cross and rub against each other. Prune to maintain an open healthy shape and always prune to outward facing buds.

Light pruning: Remove the tips of leaders (main stems) or laterals (side shoots) to stimulate new shoots and bud development. Usually done in spring.
Removing dead blooms from flowering shrubs and herbaceous plants (dead heading) is a form of light pruning.

Hard pruning: Cut back laterals or leaders to about one third or a quarter of their length, to stimulate strong new growth from the base of the plant or shoot. Usually done in autumn or winter when flowering or fruiting is over.

Moderate pruning: Cut back laterals or leaders to about two thirds or a half of their length.

Trimming: Lightly prune hedges and shrubby perennials (e.g. Helianthemum) to encourage new growth from the base and prevent the plant becoming leggy.

How to prune: Cut cleanly, using a sharp knife or secateurs. Cut immediately above an outward-facing bud or eye. Do not leave snags or stumps.

Notes

May

The weather can be deceptive; while days are usually warmer, unexpected night frosts are still possible and can damage new shoots.

Generally
Continue watering and mulching in dry weather.
Keep weeding while weeds are soft and young. Hoe round fruit and vegetables.

Sow
Basil, Chervil, Dill and any other hardy annuals.
Continue sowing vegetables.

Plant or transplant
Early Chrysanthemums.
Dahlia tubers mid-month.

Prune
Summer-prune stone fruit grown as fans or cordons.
Clip Bay trees.
Clip Privet and Lonicera nitida hedges, and continue regular trimming.

Take cuttings
Marjoram, Rosemary, Sage and Thyme.

Dress and fertilize
Lilac to encourage flowering (remove suckers).
Mulch all fruit.

Pests and diseases
Spray roses against greenfly, blackspot and mildew.
Spray apples and pears with lime-sulphur at beginning of month ('Pink Bud' stage), at end of month with Gamma-HCH (at petal fall).

Notes on weed control
Weeds compete with plants for space and light, moisture and food. Newly-planted subjects are particularly vulnerable. Weeding is boring and arduous, but early action in the spring will pay off later on. Clear all new beds before planting and weed scrupulously in the spring before roots take hold.

A 7.5 cm (3 inch) mulch around newly-planted shrubs and trees will suppress weeds. Spent mushroom compost is cheaper than peat.

Hand weed or use a hand hoe among seedlings. Use a long-handled hoe to control weeds among border plants, shrubs and trees.

Planting small, spreading ground-cover plants among larger shrubs is a good way of excluding weeds. Sowing annuals might be another, though temporary, solution.

Chemical weedkillers
Use these only as a last resort and always read labels carefully. Store well away from children.

Contact herbicides destroy leaves and stems of annual weeds, but not perennial or deep-rooting weeds.

Soil-acting selective weedkillers destroy roots and perennial weeds, eg dock, but may damage some shrubs.

Soil-acting total weedkillers do just as they say and kill everything – they may remain in the soil for up to 12 months.

Notes

June

Time to buy bedding plants and plant out pots and hanging-baskets, etc.

Generally
Water well in hot weather.
Dead-head flowers and flowering shrubs.
Weed and hoe round all plants. Pull out Sycamore seedlings now.

Sow
Hardy biennials for next year: Wallflowers, Foxglove, Polyanthus, Forget-me-not, Parsley.

Plant or transplant
Broccoli, Brussels sprouts, leeks, tomatoes on prepared site and dress with fertilizer.

Prune
Early-flowering Broom (hard), Lilac, Deutzia.
Trim Aubretia and other shrubby rock plants after flowering.
Summer-prune gooseberries, redcurrants and outdoor grape vines.

Fruit
Root strawberry runners (to be severed in 6 weeks time), by pegging down plantlet into the soil.
Thin out fruits on trees and bushes if too many, to avoid 'June Drop'.

Harvest
Early carrots, lettuce, early peas and shallots (these will keep if stored in a dry, cool place).

Notes on watering and mulching
Plants need moisture to prevent wilting and to supply them with nutrients from the soil, which they absorb in solution through their root hairs.

In very dry hot weather, regular and thorough watering is essential. Pay special attention to new plants whose root systems have not yet become established.

Water early morning or evening when it is cooler. Use a watering can with rose, hose with spray or sprinkler attachment. Leaving a sprinkler on for a couple of hours, morning or evening, will ensure that the plants are properly watered.

In drought conditions you can actually do more harm by inadequate watering than by not watering at all, since the roots are drawn up to the dry surface rather than down towards the water table.

Mulches: A mulch is a layer of organic matter spread around trees, shrubs, roses or perennials to a depth of 7.5 cm (3 inches) – any less won't stop weeds. It may be well-rotted manure, garden compost, peat or spent mushroom compost. Its functions are to retain moisture, provide food and suppress weeds.

Notes

July

Hopefully the garden is full of flowers. Keep watering, hoeing and spraying against pests and diseases.

Sow
Biennials if not done last month.
Vegetables for a continuous supply.

Plant
Belladonna Lily, Nerine, Autumn crocus (Colchicum), Snowdrop bulbs.

Prune
Early-flowering shrubs and climbers, e.g. Philadelphus (Mock Orange), Chaenomeles, Wisteria.
Summer-prune apples and pears grown as cordons.
Trim Helianthemum.
Dead-head flowers to encourage new buds.

Take cuttings
Buddleia alternifolia, Camellia japonica, Hibiscus, Winter Jasmine.
Layer Carnations and Pinks, separate after 6 weeks and transplant 3 or 4 weeks later.

Feed
Roses with rose fertilizer.
Tomatoes, if grown in tubs or pots.

Pests and diseases
Spray against aphids and whitefly everywhere.
Spray roses against greenfly, blackspot, mildew, rust.
Tie sacking bands round apple trees to catch codlin moth.

Harvest
Soft fruit, a few early potatoes, courgettes, garlic (lift, dry and store).

Notes on cuttings
Taking cuttings is a cheap and usually easy way of increasing your stock of plants. Cuttings may be made from leaf, stem or root. The most usual is the simple stem cutting, in which a section of stem is cut from the plant and inserted in soil. The cut stem forms a scar tissue at its base from which roots grow. A hormone rooting powder will speed the rooting process.

Conditions required are a warm moist atmosphere, sandy soil and a position in light but out of direct sunlight. You can root the cuttings in either a propagating case or a pot covered with a plastic bag and supported with a bent wire inside.

Cuttings like to be close together: insert 4 or 5 around the outside of a 7.5 cm (3 inch) pot. When the cuttings show signs of growth, remove the cover and pot on.

Notes

August

If you haven't gone on holiday, enjoy your roses and harvest your produce.

Generally
Continue watering.
Dead-head flowers and tidy up: dead vegetable matter encourages pests.
Take cuttings.
Continue spraying against pests and diseases.

Sow
New lawns late in the month.

Plant
Daffodil bulbs.
Separate and plant rooted strawberry runners.

Prune
Early-fruiting raspberry canes that have finished for the summer to within 15 cm (6 inches) of the ground, and any weak new canes.
Blackcurrants after fruiting (as for climbing rose – see opposite).
Trim Lavender.

Notes on roses
Roses need an open position in full sun. Autumn planting is best. They will grow in most ordinary garden soil, but do best in one which is well-dug and manured. Add compost, peat or bonemeal to the top spit before planting, and make subsequent dressings every spring. Feed with a rose fertilizer in July.

Types and their pruning
For all types the rules of standard pruning apply (see April) – that is, pruning to maintain the health of the plant. Beyond that, degrees and times of pruning vary according to the type.

Bush roses: Modern Hybrid Teas, dwarf bedding varieties and Floribundas. In all cases prune hardest the first winter or spring after planting, if not already done by the nursery.

On HTs and others, cut all growth back to a bud about 7.5 cm (3 inches) above ground level. On Floribundas, cut all growth back to a bud about 15 cm (6 inches) above ground level. Always cut to an outward facing eye.

Thereafter, prune to keep the open shape of the bush; prune vigorous young growth moderately, old basal growth harder.

Prune between December and March, depending on the weather.

Ramblers: Generally, these grow long flexible canes from the base each year. Prune old flowering stems to the base after flowering and tie in new growths. Prune after flowering has finished, about September.

Climbers: These may be Climbing H.Ts or floribundas and growth may be partly from the base and partly from higher up the stem. Prune side shoots moderately, to about two thirds of their length. Do this in early spring. Do not prune at planting time.

Notes

September

Preparing for autumn – the beginning of the digging and planting season.

Generally
Continue to harvest fruit and vegetables and tidy up.
Dig over any vacant ground or new planting areas planned. Dig in manure, compost and peat if necessary.

Plant
Late Hyacinth, Crocus, Muscari, Iris reticulata, Scilla, Chionodoxa, Leucojum (snowdrop) bulbs.
Bulbs in pots for indoors.
Paeonies and Clematis.
Layered Carnations (see July).

Take cuttings
Climbing and rambler roses – mature shoots.
Floribunda and Hybrid Teas – this year's growth.

Fertilizing
Apply autumn fertilizer to lawns.

Tidy up
All leaf and dead plant material.
Make compost heap.

Notes on the compost heap
Making a compost heap is simply a method of piling up organic waste – usually vegetable – so as to generate heat and accelerate the natural process of decomposition. It is a very good way of returning nutrients to the soil and makes an excellent mulch or dressing for the topsoil. However, you need space and a continuous supply of suitable waste to feed it with. The faster the pile can be built up, the greater the amount of heat generated, the quicker and better the results.

Use small soft leaves, young stems, flowers, annual weeds, peelings, eggshells and so on; in other words, any material which decomposes easily. Small quantities of lawn mowings are fine – thick layers tend to block air and turn to slime.

Don't use woody stems, thick or evergreen leaves, perennial weeds or anything diseased. Burn these and add the sieved ashes to the heap if you like.

Most fallen leaves are too coarse to be of much use in the compost heap; put soft leaves in a separate pile to form leaf-mould.

The compost heap must stand in shade. It needs to be contained and to have air circulating round and under it. Make a wooden-sided box or a frame with polythene sheeting stretched across it and build the pile on a bed of rubble or bricks. Compost piled in a corner will become sour and attract snails and other pests.

Make alternate layers of garden rubbish about 15 cm (6 inches) thick and thin layers of soil or manure. Pile to a maximum height of 1.2 m (4 feet) and cover with black polythene, leaving space between the top of the pile and the cover. Leave for about 3 months before using. The result should be a dark and crumbly homogenous mass with no trace of the original ingredients.

Proprietory 'activators' can be used to speed up the process.

Notes

October

In cold weather bring in all frost-sensitive plants, such as Pelargonium (geranium). Continue to dig and prepare the soil for planting.

Dig and fertilize
All new beds.
Vegetable plots – dig deeply and incorporate manure into the bottom spit.
Mulch established beds with leaf mould or compost.

Plant or transplant
Deciduous trees, shrubs, roses and climbers.
Hardy border plants.
Spring bedding plants (Wallflower, Sweet William, Polyanthus).
Continue to plant bulbs as for September (not Tulips).

Divide
Overgrown clumps of herbaceous plants, using strong outer shoots, and replant.

Prune
Fruited blackberry canes back to the ground.
Trim Iris leaves by about a quarter.
Continue dead-heading.

Lawns
Aerate and rake with springback rake.
Lay turf for new lawns.

Notes on digging and fertilizing
The main purposes of digging are to break up compacted areas of soil, improve drainage and air circulation by loosening the particles, and incorporate plant food in the form of well-rotted manure or compost.

One of the most important points to remember when digging over an area is never to mix the topsoil (top, fertile layer) with the subsoil (solid, relatively infertile layer beneath).

For this reason it is best to work methodically across an area, digging a series of trenches the depth of your spade and filling each with the soil from the previous row, mixed with manure.

Organic foods
Among the best and most easily obtained are animal manure (cow, horse, pig or poultry), garden compost, spent mushroom compost, leaf mould. These feed and improve the physical structure of the soil. They are generally slow-acting and long-lasting in effect. Dig into the soil in autumn and winter and apply as a dressing or mulch in spring.

Peat is useful as a soil conditioner and lightener of clay soils, but has little intrinsic food value.

Chemical fertilizers
Usually used to correct specific deficiencies in the soil and restore essential chemical constituents. They are fast-acting and easy to use but not long-lasting in effect. Unless you know something about the subject, use a compound form of general fertilizer which supplies the essentials in a balanced formula.

Bonemeal is an effective and slow-acting fertilizer which can be used as a dressing around shrubs in autumn and winter. Its effect is alkaline, so do not use on lime-hating shrubs like Rhododendron or Camellia.

Notes

November

Any plants you have ordered should be beginning to arrive. The main planting month. Fork over all prepared beds.

Plant
All deciduous trees and shrubs, fruit and roses.
Tulip bulbs.

Tidy up
Cut down the decayed stems of herbaceous plants and add to the compost heap. Rake and gather leaves. Burn or make a pile for leaf mould (see September).

Dig
Any unoccupied ground and leave over winter for frosts to break down.

Fruit
Remove sacking bands from apple trees and burn.

Notes on planting
Planting is best done in 'open' weather, when the ground is not heavily frosted and the soil moist but not sodden.

When the plants arrive, soak thoroughly any containers which are dry and put bare-rooted plants in a bucket of lukewarm water.

Assuming that the ground is ready, dig a hole deep enough and wide enough to take the roots or soil ball. Remove polythene covers carefully and place the plant in the hole with a sprinkling of bonemeal. Fill in and firm the soil with your hand or foot.

If the plant requires staking, add the stake while the hole is still open, to avoid damaging the roots. In the case of bare-rooted plants, such as roses, trim off any damaged roots, fan the roots out carefully and place the plants in the hole, holding with one hand and crumbling soil (with added peat if liked) around the roots with the other. Fill in and make sure not to plant above the nursery soil level. Firm the soil well with your foot.

In heavy frost, plants may have to be stored. Leave them in their packing and store in a shed or sheltered position outside. After a few days loosen the packing around the branches, but not the roots.

If the weather is suitable but the ground is not ready, 'heel in': dig a rough trench, lay in the roots and cover.

Notes

December

The beginning of a short resting period, in the garden at least. But keep an eye on newly planted shrubs, protect tender plants against bad weather and make sure young trees are firmly tied to their stakes.

Plant
Shrubs and trees in 'open' weather and dress with bonemeal.
Plant garlic bulbs, using the outer cloves, and shallot sets.

Protect
Tender plants and newly-planted evergreens with leaves or straw, e.g. Camellia.

Fruit
Winter-pruning can begin on apple, pear, gooseberry and redcurrant.

Notes

Year Round Colour in the Garden

The letters in brackets refer to types of plants. The letters after the brackets describe the main reason for growing them.

(B) = **bulb** (HB) = **hardy border plant** (S) = **shrub** (C) = **climber**
(T) = **tree** F = **flower** L = **leaf** B = **berry**

January
Chimonanthus(S)F
Eranthis(B)F
Galanthus(B)F
Hamamelis(S)F
Helleborus niger(HB)F
Jasminum nudiflorum(C)F
Mahonia(S)F
Pyracantha(S)B

February
Chionodoxa(B)F
Cornus mas(S)F
Crocus(B)F
Daphne mezereum(S)F
Garrya elliptica(S)F
Iris reticulata(B)F
Lonicera fragrantissima(S)F

May
Achillea(HB)F
Aquilegia(HB)F
Azalea(S)F
Campanula(HB)F
Choisya(S)F
Dicentra(HB)F
Laburnum(T)F
Paeonia(HB)F
Phlox subulata(HB)F

June
Alchemilla mollis(HB)F
Geranium(HB)F
Hebe(S)F
Hypericum(HB)F
Philadephus(S)F
Rose(S)F
Verbascum(HB)F

September
Anemone japonica(HB)F
Campsis(C)F
Chrysanthemum(HB)F
Clematis(C)F
Dahlia(HB)F
Parthenocissus(C)L
Rhus(S)L
Rose(S)F

October
Acer(S)L
Amaryllis(B)F
Amelanchier(S)L
Cotoneaster(S)B
Crataegus(T)B
Nerine(B)F
Prunus(T)L
Sorbus(T)L

March
Camellia(S)F
Chaenomeles(S)F
Forsythia(S)F
Hyacinth(B)F
Magnolia stellata(S)F
Muscari(B)F
Narcissus(B)F
Spiraea thunbergii(S)F

April
Amelanchier(S)F
Aubretia(HB)F
Convallaria(HB)F
Cytisus praecox(S)F
Leucojum(B)F
Prunus(T)F
Rhododendron(S)F
Tulip(B)F

July
Astilbe(HB)F
Clematis(C)F
Helianthemum(HB)F
Kniphofia(HB)F
Lavandula(S)F
Mimulus(HB)F
Potentilla(S)F
Salvia(S)F

August
Fuchsia(S)F
Hibiscus(S)F
Hydrangea(S)F
Montbretia(HB)F
Olearia(S)F
Passiflora(C)F
Solidago(HB)F

November
Berberis thunbergii(S)L
Cornus kousa(S)L
Cyclamen alpinum(B)F
Gentiana(HB)F
Malus(T)L
Schizostylis(B)F
Skimmia(S)B
Symphoricarpos(S)B
Viburnum(S)L

December
Chimonanthus(S)F
Cornus(S)L and stem
Elaeagnus(S)L
Erica carnea(S)F
Ilex(S)B
Iris unguicularis(B)F

Useful Addresses

Keep a note here of the names and addresses of well-stocked garden centres and nurseries and any other useful suppliers.

Name Address	Telephone

Name Address	Telephone